A Member Is Worth a Thousand Visitors

"In recent decades, publishing has undergone a seismic shift. The explosion of free online content, the growth of online advertising megaliths, and the Great Recession eroded traditional revenue streams and left many publishers feeling rudderless.

In this book, Rob helps niche media companies 'get their groove back' by outlining five well-supported methods to stabilized revenue and move away from legacy online advertising and print publishing. If you're considering the move to a subscription or membership model (and you should be!), this book will serve as a strategic compass."

—Elizabeth Peterson, President of H3.Group and Board Member of the Specialized Information Publishers Association

"You don't need a technical background to use Rob's easy-to-employ money-making approaches. This book will drive radically higher rates of revenue for you by providing strategies to engage key customers and attract new ones."

—Chuck Croft, CEO of DRG and Annie's Publishing

"While everyone else is taking the same stale approaches, Rob Ristagno has written the essential state-of-the-art playbook for selling content online."

—Brian Cuthbert, Group Vice President of Diversified Communications

"I've been in publishing for decades and I don't think there has ever been a concept that excites me more than paid membership communities. Most publishers have spent years and invested countless resources into building their brand, developing a community or tribe around a common interest or passion, and it's time to double-down on the concept. Thanks, Rob!"

—Wes Buck, Founder and Editor, *Drag Illustrated*

A
MEMBER
IS WORTH A
THOUSAND
VISITORS

A PROVEN METHOD FOR MAKING
MORE MONEY ONLINE

ROB RISTAGNO

STERLINGWOODSGROUP.COM

Copyright © 2018 by Rob Ristagno

For more information contact:
Rob Ristagno
209 Elliot St
Newton, MA 02464 USA
+1 617 544 7883
https://robristagno.com

Printed in the United States of America.

ISBN Paperback: 9781980406716
Copyright: 2018938870

Interior Design: Dotti Albertine

*Dedicated
to my daughter
Helena Jo*

CONTENTS

MANY PUBLISHERS ARE trapped in a vicious circle of cutting costs and losing revenue. They're stuck wondering, "How can I cut another penny from my production cost so I can meet payroll?" instead of, "What big, new change can I make to grow my business?"

It puts them in a stressful situation, operating day to day—it feels like the industry is crumbling around them, and they have to struggle to keep their doors open. Print is declining, which makes many publishers feel they don't have options to grow. Meanwhile, the Internet gobbles up their readership and social media conglomerates siphon off their ad revenue.

The Internet and the digital world can be overwhelming for many publishers. They don't have time to collect and process data. They don't feel like their teams can move fast enough to keep up with technology.

Their leaders feel trapped putting out fires all day long, instead of feeling empowered to direct the strategy of the business. It's understandable. It can be hard to adapt to an ever-changing landscape, especially as popular culture declares over and over that print is dead.

But you can break the cycle and thrive in this new environment. You can leave behind all those concerns about squeezing an extra penny out of every issue, and move on to a prosperous future. Content creators and publishers can achieve double-digit growth, year after year, while confidently creating great content. Wouldn't it be great to make a lot more money and be more focused on growth?

In this book, I will help you quickly and effectively refocus on the *five essential forces* you can use to steer out of the weeds, grow your business, and once again act with confidence. I will make the Internet accessible for people who've been accustomed to another medium and don't know how to adapt.

Here's the thing: If you're a content creator, you're sitting on a gold mine. You have two huge assets in the digital world: great content and a thriving community. Nearly everyone is trying to generate those two things. If you have one or both already, you're way ahead of the game. All you need to do is monetize them.

That's where I come in. I have dedicated my career to applying the industry-leading business principles I learned at Harvard Business School and McKinsey & Company to helping small and medium-sized content creators and publishers grow.

My goal in writing this book is to help great content creators harness the power of digital strategies to earn double-digit returns. Just as important, I will help you focus on the right elements of your business so you can gain control of your destiny.

By following the lessons in this book, you can transform your company, and go from cutting expenses and hoping to keep your doors open to growing revenue by leaps and bounds. You can transform the Internet from a threat into a powerful tool for making money online.

Who can benefit from this? I'm writing this book primarily for owners and senior executives of firms that produce high-quality, specialized content. While I focus primarily on publishers, these lessons apply to *any* small or medium-sized business that produces written content, podcasts, videos, or print. That could include niche publishers, consultants, motivational speakers, personal trainers, authors, entertainment companies, data aggregators, or content marketers.

Many people get involved in content creation because they're passionate about what they're creating. If you implement the right business strategy and technology—which I will show you how to do in this book—you will make more money, and you'll have more time to focus on what you love doing: creating great content that engages your community. You will replace the vicious circle of shaving expenses and pumping out high-quantity, low-quality content with a virtuous circle of creating more amazing content and connecting with your fans in a way that allows you to thrive no matter how technology changes.

I invite you to come along with me for this journey.

CHAPTER ONE

FORGET THE BARNACLES —FOLLOW THE WHALES!

CONSUMERS ALL WANT quality content, yet very few companies that produce good content monetize it effectively. Too many companies focus on broadening their audience to garner ad revenue, when they should be doing the opposite. If your audience is a niche market, trying to compete with massive companies for eyeballs and ad revenue will not work.

The truth for small to mid-sized publishers is this: **You have to stop relying on advertising**. Advertising can be a piece of your revenue puzzle, but it cannot sustain your business alone.

Why not?

Well, marketers are redeploying their ad spends away from traditional media, especially print. Why are they doing that? *They want to keep their jobs.*

They know they won't get fired for investing in digital—but they might get fired for investing in print, which many marketers regard as a dinosaur. Self-preservation is a powerful motivator, and it drives marketers to purchase digital ads.

Now, you might think that all you have to do is migrate your content online, and you'll be able to keep the same advertising clients. Unfortunately for content creators, most advertisers are not giving their money to digital publishers, either. They're giving it to Google and Facebook, which now account for 60 percent of all Internet advertising, while no other company in the US market has more than a 5 percent market share.[1]

The conglomerates' share of the pie is only growing. As giants like Google and Facebook improve their advertising platforms and draw more eyeballs to their sites using others' content (including yours!), they continue to gain a larger share of the total advertising pie.

The top thirty companies that earn ad revenue (including TV, digital, and print ads) now control 44 percent of all ad revenue—up from 33 percent in 2012.[2] This consolidation of revenue by the top companies will continue to grow, because they get more sophisticated by the day at targeting the right audience. In doing so, the behemoths draw more ad dollars away from publishers and into their coffers.

[1] "Why Google and Facebook Prove the Digital Ad Market Is a Duopoly," *Fortune*, July 28, 2017 (via Reuters), http://fortune.com/2017/07/28/google-facebook-digital-advertising/.
[2] Rani Molla, "Google and Facebook Are Driving Nearly All Growth in the Global Ad Market," *recode*, May 2, 2017, https://www.recode.net/2017/5/2/15516674/global-ad-spending-charts.

Simply put, Google and Facebook can provide advertisers better analytics, and marketers are getting savvier, demanding more data from advertising platforms than simply number of visitors.

The old adage "I know that 50 percent of my marketing works; I just don't which 50," is no longer true. Google and Facebook can tell them exactly how much ROI they receive for each dollar spent.

Meanwhile, there's no way to prove that banner ads on your website really "build a brand" for your advertisers. That makes it hard for you to compete with companies that can show them their advertising ROI (which they can use to show their bosses how well they're doing—so they get promoted rather than fired).

Do you really want to compete with Google and Facebook in creating marketing ROI analytics?

Advertising is simply not enough to sustain a content business anymore.

How the World Has Changed

Not only has the world moved away from print while ad dollars have moved to Google and Facebook, but there's just a lot more content online.

A lot of people try to fight the glut of content out there by being annoying—sending out way too many e-mails, pumping out tons of low-quality content, and jamming their websites with irritating pop-ups, banners, and auto-playing video ads. These things ruin the user experience.

Most of the industry is trapped in this vicious circle, creating content of lower and lower quality that drives consumers and advertisers away.

However, there is another way, which I will show you in this book. In fact, **you can use your competitors' degrading user experience as an opportunity.**

People are sick of annoying banner and pop-up ads. They're sick of low-quality content and listicles like "The top five ways that WHO CARES." You can take advantage of that. You can be a safe haven for your users—a place where they can get exactly the content they want without having their experience disrupted by obnoxious promotions. People will pay you to escape the deluge of low-quality content they find online.

You Can Grow Even as Advertising Revenue Declines

You **do not** have to downsize as advertising revenue drops—**you can still experience double-digit revenue growth consistently, year after year,** as my clients have done, even while their industries at large have suffered.

The shift to digital is an *opportunity* for the publishing world—not a threat. This book will give you the strategies you need to take advantage of that opportunity.

I've applied the techniques in this book to help niche publishers unleash their profound (but hidden) market strengths and rich content archives, enabling them to lock in growth of 50 percent or more, year after year.

Through my experience helping publishers grow, I've developed a proven system that employs **five forces** you can control to refocus your business and marketing to systematically boost sales and profits. Publishers who embark on this journey find it liberating, because for the first time in years they feel truly focused—they know what they need to do to succeed, and how to do it.

What can happen for niche publishers that apply these principles? **Established publishers can see revenue boosts of 50 to 600 percent**, and new publishers can generate six-figure revenue in their first year.

A Paywall Is Essential—But Not Enough

The first thing you have to accept is that you MUST put up a paywall and create a membership model around your content (we'll get into the difference between a paywall and a membership model in chapter 2). Putting up a paywall is essential, but it isn't enough, especially if it's done suddenly and without a comprehensive business strategy.

You have to do it the right way. I will teach you the five principles you need to follow to execute a successful paywall strategy. Only once you are ready to implement all five forces should you embark on creating a paywall. All five of these forces are based on a single, foundational principle: you must find your best customers—or as I call them, your "whales"—and focus *relentlessly* on their wants and needs.

(A quick clarification on my use of the words *customer* and *consumer*. Because the teachings in this book apply to both B2B and B2C business, for simplicity, I'll use the term *customer* to mean someone who gives you money: either an individual or business buyer. When I say "consumer," I mean anyone who utilizes your content; again, this could be either an individual or a business. Thus, you can read the terms *customer* and *consumer* somewhat interchangeably.)

Why Is It So Important to Identify and Cater to Your Whales?

Whales are the key to unlocking explosive growth in the digital world. Simply put, your whales in aggregate account for the vast majority of your revenue. This is true in any business. Across industries, the top 10 percent of customers drive 30 to 70 percent of sales.

Whales provide the following value to your business:

- They are less price-sensitive, which makes them more profitable.
- They buy more often.
- They want to help you innovate.
- They provide word-of-mouth marketing— inspiring other customers to come to you.
- They behave more predictably.

Dollar Shave Club rode their whales all the way to a billion dollars within five years. They targeted eighteen- to thirty-year-old men and focused on a few of their pain points: Many young men cannot afford Gillette razors. They like shopping online, and they hate going out to buy razors—or even worse, forgetting to do so.

Dollar Shave Club created a good-enough product to meet the needs and price point of their customers, and started a subscription razor blade program (which was convenient for customers and helped DSC achieve predictable, consistent revenue), and reached their whales with great marketing. Dollar Shave Club exploded onto the scene in 2012, and sold to Unilever in 2016 for a ***billion dollars***.[3]

They achieved that enormous success by focusing exclusively on their whales and offering a *specific* product that their whales were willing to pay for.

Casinos build their success on the backs of their whales—indeed, *whale* as a business term was coined as a reference to the high rollers on whom the casino industry's business model is focused. Wynn Resorts, for example, keeps a list of their 50,000 highest rollers, and they do everything they can to make those people happy. Client managers are paid as much as $5 million a year just to manage these high rollers—the biggest and most important whales.

Why do they focus on this niche, rather than attracting as many people as they can to the casino? After all, tens of millions of gamblers come to Las Vegas—these 50,000 high rollers are far less than one percent of all potential customers.

---

[3] Jaclyn Trop, "How Dollar Shave Club's Founder Built a $1 Billion Company That Changed the Industry," *Entrepreneur*, March 28, 2017, https://www.entrepreneur.com/article/290539#.

They do it because the whales drive massive growth for them. By catering specifically to them, a casino can give them *everything* they'd ever want to spend gobs of money on. They go there because they know they'll get exactly what they want. And not only do they bring their large checkbooks with them, they also bring the "fish"— the wannabe whales who strive to be like the high rollers.

By expertly serving this very small percentage of the total market, Wynn Resorts and other casinos created a very successful business. And yet, many publishers and content creators take the opposite approach. They don't look for their high rollers; they're just trying to attract as large a crowd as possible. They don't care who is in that crowd—they just want eyeballs. They want traffic. They are willing to give their content away for free to attract more people, because their entire focus is on advertisers.

That doesn't work.

Content creators need to identify their whales and serve their needs as best they can. Rather than trying to get more eyeballs, you should look for ways to carve off a small percentage of the total potential audience and laser-focus on providing a service that they are willing to pay for.

The Three Types of Customers

Your customers can be broken down into three types.

Whales: Your most engaged and enthusiastic customers. Whales make up about 20 percent of the audience and typically provide 80 percent of the revenue. Not only that, whales also influence fish to come into your boat, some of whom may become whales over time.

Fish: Fish represent a large portion of your customer base, but each fish does not provide a ton of revenue. Fish may make up roughly 40 percent of your readership/viewership and around 20 percent of your revenue. The hope with fish is that the cachet you earn from serving the whales, plus favorable word of mouth from the whales themselves, may lead to some of your fish becoming whales over time.

Barnacles: Barnacles are a large segment of your readership/viewership—and they cling to your boat without ever spending a cent. Barnacles may be up to 40 percent of your audience, but you should not focus on attracting them, because they generate zero direct revenue for your business.

They may be a key piece of your advertising strategy *for now*, but as advertisers get savvier, they'll realize that these people aren't worth anything to them either and will stop paying to reach them.

For example, one publisher I talked to made a point to keep their e-mail list numbers high because the size of the list was a selling point for ads. But when we looked at the list, we found that 40 percent of the names were not actual people; they were addresses like info@ companyname.com, or salesteam@companyname.com (there were even some R-rated e-mail addresses that would make you blush!).

So, while advertisers paid based on the size of their list, eventually they were bound to realize that the real economic value of those leads was zero. I explained to them that it was only a matter of time before advertisers wised up and decided to only pay for opens, or clicks— effectively ending the value of the barnacles to this company.

Focusing on Your Whales Is Vital for Content Creators

Focusing on your whales is key in any industry, but for content creators, it's arguably even more crucial. That's because approximately **40 out of every 100 people will never pay a penny for content**. No matter how good your content is, that's just the reality. As a result, whales are responsible for an enormous percentage of revenue in content businesses.

In the mobile gaming industry (a content industry), 37 percent of users never spend any money (the barnacles). They download the free version of the game and never purchase anything. However, that's okay for game producers, because the top 1 percent of users generate 20 percent of the revenue, and the top 20 percent of users generate a whopping 88 percent of the revenue. In short, the whales support the entire industry. *(page 23)*

As a content creator, you have to stop thinking about how you can get one million more people to look at your page so that you can charge an advertiser more money. No matter how many people are coming to your site, advertisers will still primarily spend on Facebook and Google, because they have more eyeballs than you do, and they can target specific audience segments extremely well.

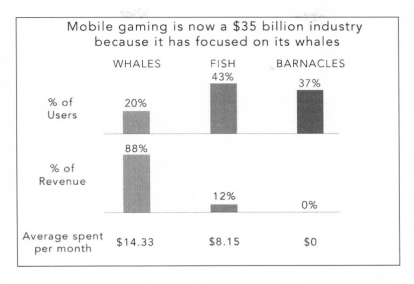

Mobile gaming is now a $35 billion industry because it has focused on its whales

	WHALES	FISH	BARNACLES
% of Users	20%	43%	37%
% of Revenue	88%	12%	0%
Average spent per month	$14.33	$8.15	$0

However, you *can* be super focused on **your** best customers—the small percentage of your base that actually drives revenue—and provide a better experience for them in your niche than they can get anywhere else. They will pay for your service, and you will earn more money and have happier customers.

Furthermore, if you do a good job with your whales, you'll see more of your "fish" become whales, because the fish look up to the whales and want to follow in their footsteps.

If you can do that, you can lock in double-digit revenue growth even as your competitors drop off around you. I've helped my clients thrive in "declining markets," and seen large companies do the same.

The *New York Times* pulled itself from the brink of bankruptcy by switching its strategy from relying on advertising to increasing subscription revenue.

Twenty years ago, advertising accounted for 63 percent of the *New York Times'* revenue, while subscriptions contributed 27 percent. However, after advertising revenue cratered for the paper—as it did for much of the industry in the mid 2000s—the *Times* changed its approach. The paper put up a paywall and focused on digital subscriptions. Today, its revenue ratio has flipped: Subscriptions are now responsible for 61 percent of revenue, while ad revenue makes up 33 percent.[4] Subscription revenues have in fact just exceeded $1 billion for the Gray Lady.[5]

The *New York Times* survived because it understood what makes its core readers tick and how they wanted to consume content, and the paper gave it to them for a price.

What the *Times* did can be applied to small publishers too. In fact, there is a start-up business right now that is rapidly growing into a powerhouse directly at the expense of larger companies. That publisher is *The Athletic*, and it has achieved this success by creating great content, focusing on its whales, and charging for access.

The Athletic launched in January 2016, and in less than two years it has become one of the largest sports media companies in the United States. The company's

---

[4] https://www.recode.net/2017/5/4/15550052/new-york-times-subscription-advertising-revenue-chart.
[5] "Rethinking News: Inside The New York Times Digital Subscriptions Explosion," Sterling Woods Blog, February 20, 2018, https://sterlingwoodsgroup.com/blog/nyt-digital-subscriptions/.

approach was simple: target local newspapers' whales—sports fans.

The founders of *The Athletic* told the *New York Times* that they "believe that sports is an undervalued part of that bundle (newspapers), and that there are tens of thousands of sports fans in each city who don't care about the other sections, and would rather jettison their subscription and pay for *The Athletic* instead."[6]

While local newspapers were laying off sportswriters to save money, *The Athletic* saw an opportunity—scoop up sports journalism talent and cater exclusively to sports fans by providing excellent local stories, which they know their customers are willing to pay for. *The Athletic* focuses exclusively on delivering a great experience for their whales, and it's working. They charge sports fans sixty dollars a year for access to great content and a safe haven from the ad-destroyed reading experience offered by many major sports sites today.

Compare the reader's experience for these two screenshots: one has a clean interface, similar to subscription sites like *The Athletic*, and the other has pop-ups, banner ads, auto-playing videos, and more disruptions, like many mass-media sports sites. *(page 26)*

In the second screenshot *(page 27)*, a visitor hoping to read an article sees multiple ads, with distracting

---

[6] Kevin Draper, "Why The Athletic Wants to Pillage Newspapers," New York Times, October 23, 2017, https://www. nytimes.com/2017/10/23/sports/the-athletic-newspapers. html?smid=tw-nytsports&smtyp=cur.

The Article You Want to Read

consectetur adipisci velit

December 13, 2017

By Jane Doe

There are no ads or distractions interrupting your reading experience! Enjoy the clean page, your sole refuge from popups and banner ads! Ut enim ad minim veniam, quis nostrud exercitation ullamco laboris nisi ut aliquip ex ea commodo consequat. Duis aute irure dolor in reprehenderit in voluptate velit esse cillum dolore eu fugiat nulla pariatur. Excepteur sint occaecat cupidatat non proident, sunt in culpa qui officia deserunt mollit anim id est laborum.

Sed ut perspiciatis unde omnis iste natus error sit voluptatem accusantium doloremque laudantium, totam rem aperiam, eaque ipsa quae ab illo inventore veritatis et quasi architecto beatae vitae dicta sunt explicabo. Nemo enim ipsam voluptatem quia voluptas sit aspernatur aut odit aut fugit, sed quia consequuntur magni dolores eos qui ratione voluptatem sequi nesciunt. Neque porro quisquam est, qui dolorem ipsum quia dolor sit amet, consectetur, adipisci velit, sed quia non numquam eius modi tempora incidunt ut labore et dolore magnam aliquam quaerat voluptatem. Ut enim ad minima veniam, quis nostrum exercitationem ullam corporis suscipit laboriosam, nisi ut aliquid ex ea commodi consequatur? Quis autem vel eum iure reprehenderit qui in ea voluptate velit esse quam nihil molestiae consequatur, vel illum qui dolorem eum fugiat quo voluptas nulla.

SHARE SHARE Catchy Headline for
An Article You Want to Read

Catchy Headline for An Article You Want to Read

By Jane Doe   December 13, 2017

Sed ut perspiciatis unde omnis iste natus error sit voluptatem accusantium doloremque laudantium, totam rem aperiam, eaque ipsa quae ab illo inventore veritatis et quasi architecto beatae vitae dicta sunt explicabo. Nemo enim ipsam

Disruptive Pop-up Asking for your Email ✕

SUBMIT

videos playing (with sound that readers have to turn off), and other information that obscures nearly the entire screen—making it very difficult to actually consume the content they came for.

Meanwhile, the first screenshot is clean, uninterrupted by ads, videos, or other content the reader didn't ask for. Your whales will pay for the better experience they receive on a page like that.

The Athletic's meteoric rise proves that. Even though its subscription revenue gives them plenty of cash on hand, the company raised almost $8 million in venture capital funding to scoop up accomplished journalists who had been laid off by ad-dependent local newspapers, and to attract talent from national giants ESPN, Fox Sports, and *Sports Illustrated*.

Those companies are paying the price for their declining user experience and reliance on ad revenue, and *The Athletic* is reaping the benefits by exclusively targeting whales, creating a great user experience for them, and charging them for it. This is why a start-up like *The Athletic* is growing rapidly while giants in their market are suffering.

As I said, these strategies apply to niche publishers too. Even if your market isn't as big as "sports fans," you can maximize income online by treating your whales right! My mission is to help you do so.

Applying Big-Business Principles to Niche Publishers

My two dream jobs growing up were college professor and game show host. So as an adult, I started my own company, Sterling Woods Group, which allows me to apply elements of both of those careers to helping niche publishers master the digital world.

I get to be like a college professor, researching and teaching, taking complex subject matter and boiling it down to understandable bits that people can act on. I get to help people learn new skills and teach them things that I've researched in depth and discovered from hands-on experience helping hundreds of companies.

On the other hand, I get to apply my love of games (which made me want to become a game show host) to the vital art of A/B testing. Doing A/B testing with strategies is sort of like the show *Let's Make a Deal*. What's behind curtain one? How about curtain two? You have to actually try both to find out whether you will get zonked or get the car.

My company gives me a chance to merge my two ideal jobs with my business background to help organizations I care about grow. A lot of people with my background are not focused on small or medium-sized businesses.

I went to Harvard Business School and worked for five years at McKinsey & Company. Then I realized in my heart that I wanted to have an impact with smaller companies, so I made a career out of applying the approaches used by some of the greatest business leaders in the world to small and medium-sized businesses. That's my passion.

My Goal: To Demystify the Digital World for You
I help people who "don't know what they don't know"

about online technology focus on what they like doing/ are the best at (creating great content that engages their community), and let the technical experts take care of the technology end of things.

The digital world seems intimidating, but it doesn't need to be. Yes, there are technical aspects of it—but you can leave the technical parts up to the experts. Your role is to set a good business strategy and a clear vision.

Once you have your strategy mapped out, it's easier to specify what you need from the experts. You can delegate the technical aspects to experts the same way you trust your accountant to file your taxes every year. You don't have to be an accountant to manage an accountant.

It's the same with digital. Just as a good accountant will do a better job doing your taxes if they understand what you're trying to accomplish, if you get your strategy right, you can lay out clear expectations for your technical experts and let them handle the details.

A big secret is that a lot of the technical tools do the same thing, so picking one or the other won't make or break your business. It's far more important to map out the correct business strategy and find the tools you need based on how they fit into that strategy. You should assess your technical vendors the same way you would an accountant—by how they fit your business needs.

But you don't need to worry about the technical side just yet. Later in this book, I will give you a process to use to screen experts so you can ensure that they actually understand your business needs, and that you can therefore trust them to pick the right tool for you.

First and foremost, however, we need to focus on creating the right business strategy. Read on, and I will share with you the insights you need to master the digital world, so that you can stop putting out fires and looking for ways to shave off costs, and start earning new revenue streams and growing your business by leaps and bounds.

CHAPTER TWO

HOW TO *ACTUALLY* MAKE MONEY ONLINE

AS I EXPLAINED in chapter one, the advertising model is dying. So, logically, if you are heavily ad-supported today, you have to charge for at least some of your content. If you already charge for content, there are still challenges you have to break through to drive dramatic growth of your digital membership. Bottom line: online success requires more than simply putting up a paywall.

In this chapter I will outline the tools available to you and the mindset you need to have in order to make money online. I will debunk some common fears and provide insight into which aspects of your business you should focus on in order to monetize your content in the digital world.

Paywalls, Subscriptions, and Memberships

There are three different levels of paid content products. Let's go through all three levels, and I'll show you why you must be at level three to succeed.

Level 1: Paywall

A paywall is a way to gate your content so that it is not freely available to everyone. While this is an important part of your revenue strategy, a paywall alone will not be your salvation. You can't simply add a paywall to your existing site and expect people to start paying for your content. When publishers fail to monetize their content online, the problem is usually that they put up a paywall without a strategy or marketing plan. Putting up a paywall was a technology-driven decision. They instituted a paywall, thinking it was a *Field of Dreams* situation, that "if you build it, they will come."

That doesn't work. There's more to it than that.

Level 2: Subscription

A subscription is a business model in which you charge customers for access to your content for a set period of time, at the end of which they can choose to renew or lapse their subscriptions.

A subscriber has a transactional relationship with your company. They subscribe to the content behind a paywall, and they're a customer. You care that they come in the door, and then you worry about renewal efforts, and that's as deep as the relationship goes.

A subscription business model is an important part of what you need to do, but true success in the online world lies in the third option: a membership program.

Level 3: Membership

A membership combines the business model of a subscription with the technology of a paywall, but there's more to it than that. Creating a membership means that you are creating a community around your content, that you are understanding and meeting your audience's needs with information, inspiration, and interaction.

Members have a stronger emotional connection to your brand than subscribers do. For example, I'm a Netflix *subscriber*, but I'm a *member* of the Museum of Fine Arts. There's a big difference in the relationship between customer and company.

Customers feel proud to support services that bestow membership, like the Museum of Fine Arts, and that kind of pride isn't attached to a subscription service like Netflix. PBS supporters feel this same kind of pride: it feels to them like their membership makes this great content possible and makes them part of a community of supporters.

A membership sends a clear message: You are important. You are a member. You can brag about your membership. I'm excited to tell people, "Hey if you ever want to go to the museum, I can take you."

Who are the most devoted members of your audience, and what are they willing to pay for? What problem can your content solve for them? How can you create an outstanding user experience that allows them to discover and consume your material when and how they need to, on any device?

Memberships often offer more than basic content. Netflix just offers entertainment; the Museum of Fine Arts has tiers of benefits that go beyond simply accessing the museum, such as discounts on dining, special events, guest passes to bring friends, reciprocal admission to other museums, and opportunities to attend exhibition opening events.[7] It doesn't take much for you to turn a subscription service into a membership model, but the perceived value to the reader is enormous. The difference between being good and outstanding is very small, yet so few people go that last centimeter to stand out that the rewards are much greater for those who do. Anyone can do a *good* job, but if you put in that last, extra hour to go above and beyond and do a *great* job, you reap a disproportionate share of the rewards.

This goes beyond offering past magazine issues behind a paywall. The companies that do this the best add services, such as live help, special discounts, free shipping, etc. Think about how much cachet Amazon has added to its Prime membership: it started with free shipping, and now it includes music, movies, exclusive programming, storage space, and more.

Statista charges about $5,000 per year for access to research reports behind a paywall. The site is searchable. It's also organized in a way to make discovery easy and intuitive. Don't see what you want? Statista analysts will dig deeper for you to see if additional or updated data is available—for no extra charge.

The *Wall Street Journal* also bundles a lot of value to justify its premium online subscriptions. It includes well-curated daily e-mails tailored to your preferences,

---

[7] "Levels and Benefits," The Museum of Fine Arts, Boston, http://www.mfa.org/membership/levels-and-benefits.

effective content recommendation engines, special offers, and discounts on unique products and events. Content is easy to discover and read on a desktop, tablet, or phone.

A lot of content creators decide to charge for content and then just buy the paywall technology—and fail. Some people realize they need a subscription service, and they implement that business model ... and it fails. But those who create a membership platform—creating a community that provides inspiration and drives brand loyalty—find success online.

If you already have a paywall or a subscription model, that's great. You have a head start. But that's not enough. Read on, and we'll show you how you can better monetize it by finding and serving your whales.

How Do You Make Money with a Membership Model?

It's simple: Carve out a niche of whales, serve their needs better than anyone else, and charge them for it. Doing this doesn't mean shutting off other traffic, customers, or ad revenue. Even mass media brands can carve out a niche without sacrificing traffic.

Politico is a great example. They've created a mostly free site targeted at consumers, offering general news about politics, and generating ad revenue. They've also carved off a chunk of their audience—professional politicians—and charged them for Politico Pro.

Politico realized they were already spending resources covering politics, and they had the necessary sources and information to serve the needs of professional politicians by providing exclusive, high-value content.

They charge pro members handsomely: Membership prices range from $10,000 to $300,000 a year, and membership revenue is estimated to be somewhere north of $100 million—and their members are so happy with the product that more than 90 percent of them renew each year.[8] *Fortune* magazine explains the reason for the success of this model:

Why does *Politico*'s model work so well? Because it is a highly targeted offering that is aimed at a relatively tiny market—primarily government workers and lobbyists and analysts who focus on those issues—but it serves that market extremely well. And as a result, those readers are willing to pay a hefty sum for that information, because it adds enough value to make it worthwhile.[9]

In short, *Politico* is successful because they focus relentlessly on their whales. *Politico* monetized a niche segment of their audience while maintaining their free mass media site's traffic and ad revenue.

Politico Pro has been so successful that *Fortune* wonders why more publishers aren't taking *Politico*'s lead:

Even the most mass-market publication probably

[8] Max Willens, "How 4 of the Priciest Content Subscriptions Stack up," *Digiday*, August 10, 2017.
[9] Mathew Ingram, "Politico Pro Is a Lesson in the Benefits of a Laser-Focused Paywall," *Fortune*, August 2015, http://fortune.com/2015/08/10/politico-pro-paywall/.

has niches that could probably be useful for targeted newsletter-style publications or subscription models, whether it's financial products or sports content or analytical insight in a variety of areas. Why have so few tried to build their own *Politicos*?[10]

They're correct to ask that question, because most of the industry is leaving money on the table.

Why Membership Is So Effective

Membership is the most profitable model for many content creators, for several reasons:

First, it's a subscription product, not a one-and-done.

The problem with one-and-done products is that the revenue only occurs once. If you make one hundred sales this year, you have to make one hundred new sales next year just to maintain. Compare that to a subscription model, with which you should expect a 60–70 percent renewal rate (or more). On January 1, you have the comfort of knowing that 70 percent of last year's revenue is already booked because you have a renewal offering. You don't need huge conversion rates to grow revenue, because it snowballs: if you convert 1 percent more subscribers month after month, year after year, and renew 60 or 70 percent of them each year, it doesn't take too long for this to become a very big business.

---

[10] Mathew Ingram, "Politico Pro Is a Lesson in the Benefits of a Laser-Focused Paywall," *Fortune*, August 2015, http://fortune.com/2015/08/10/politico-pro-paywall/.

Second, you don't need a large percentage of your traffic to convert for you to make a lot of money. For example, you can charge a *single* member $60 a year (or more) for a membership; you would need more than *twenty-four thousand* visitors to generate the same $60 from Google AdSense (at an average CPM of $2.50).[11] All of that without renewals, and without the opportunity to upsell those thousand visitors. That's why the title of this book is *A Member Is Worth a Thousand Visitors* (I considered calling it *A Member Is Worth 24,000 Visitors* ... but that would have been too clunky).

Third, your marginal costs are low. Once you build the site, you're mainly repurposing information from your archives—and collecting membership fees with a healthy profit margin.

The Opportunity Is Right in Front of You

Most of the media industry is missing a huge opportunity: They have the audience and the content, but they don't recognize the revenue opportunities available to them.

Forbes is a great example. Let me start by saying I have utmost respect for this brand. But I would do things differently.

Forbes has a strong brand, credibility, and an

---

[11] Scott Bateman, "AdSense CPM Depends on Category and Tactics," Promise Media, accessed February 21, 2018, https://www.promisemedia.com/online-advertising/adsense-cpm-depends-category-tactics.

audience, but they could be doing a lot more to monetize their content. Why doesn't *Forbes* have a CEO-level digital membership product? Instead, in search of ever more elusive ad revenue, they have cluttered their user experience with clickbait and pop-ups, which is not sustainable.

Have you clicked on a Forbes.com article lately? I did, and was astonished by how rough the user experience was. When I got to the landing page, there was a site takeover, meaning that an ad for one of their advertisers covers the entire screen. I waited for the countdown to end so I could finally view the article, and distractions immediately bombarded me. A video started playing, another ad popped up, and banner ads interrupted my reading experience. (The article I clicked on was only 273 words long. That's a lot of advertising for such a short piece.)

Not only that, but their content is also not always up to par. *Forbes* positions itself as "The Capitalist Tool," providing practical resources and information to help business people perform better in their careers. Based on this promise, I'd expect rich content supported by deep investigation. Instead, I find "listicles" like these:

1. "Three Common Misconceptions About Legacy Planning"[12]

---

[12] Daniel Scott, "Three Common Misconceptions About Legacy Planning," *Forbes*, November 15, 2017, https://www.forbes.com/sites/danielscott1/2017/11/15/three-common-misconceptions-about-legacy-planning/#487af75f281e.

2. "10 Reasons The Stock Market Will Have A Good 2018"[13]

3. "The Productivity Tricks Of Seven Successful Entrepreneurs"[14]

To me, these sound like articles that should be on Buzzfeed, not Forbes.com. Not coincidentally, *Forbes* is laying off employees and scaling back publication of its print magazine.[15] On the surface, reallocating resources from a declining business (print) to the business of the future (digital) is a smart move. We've all heard cautionary tales about companies that failed to adapt to new technologies and paid the ultimate price (Blockbuster, Kodak, etc.).

However, *Forbes* is making one key misstep in my analysis. They are not simply redirecting resources away from magazines; they are giving up on **quality content creation.** They're no longer focused on creating good content and a good user experience. You can't build a membership community around clickbait and annoying ads.

---

[13] Larry Light, "10 Reasons The Stock Market Will Have A Good 2018," *Forbes*, November 20, 2017, https://www.forbes.com/sites/lawrencelight/2017/11/20/10-reasons-the-stock-market-will-have-a-good-2018/.

[14] Alison Coleman, "The Productivity Tricks Of Seven Successful Entrepreneurs," *Forbes*, November 26, 2017, https://www.forbes.com/sites/alisoncoleman/2017/11/26/the-productivity-tricks-of-seven-successful-entrepreneurs/#2f8bd34a3985.

[15] Keith J. Kelly, "Forbes Scaling Back to 10 Issues in 2018," *New York Post*, November 16, 2017, https://nypost.com/2017/11/16/forbes-scaling-back-to-10-issues-in-2018/.

Right now, Forbes.com is dependent on a contributor model in which over 2,500 bloggers provide the content for them. I don't see how you can possibly control the quality and consistency of content from 2,500 bloggers. I bet many of these writers are fantastic, but my point is it's tough to maintain quality standards if you're relying on a network of thousands of bloggers.

Forbes seems to be chasing traffic, hoping to monetize through display advertising. But they are pursuing an unsustainable strategy. As their content continues to decline in quality, and the experience becomes increasingly unbearable, their traffic and engagement will plummet.

On the plus side, *Forbes* is also starting to launch reader revenue streams. Specifically, they have a portfolio of paid-subscription investment letters that cost $200 or more per year. That's a smart move, because they're isolating an engaged segment of the audience and selling something to them, rather than relying solely on advertising. Hopefully *Forbes* will turn their focus to more products like this, rather than continuing to chase traffic and diminish their user experience with listicles and pop-ups.

If you go the clickbait route, you can kill your brand. On the other hand, if you follow in the footsteps of companies like *Politico* or *The Athletic*, and charge users for a membership that provides a great experience, you can flourish.

Niche Brands Can Succeed with a Membership Model
The idea of targeting a specific audience and meeting

their needs exceptionally well doesn't just apply to mass media brands. In fact, niche publishers actually do a better job of capitalizing on their whales via a paywall.

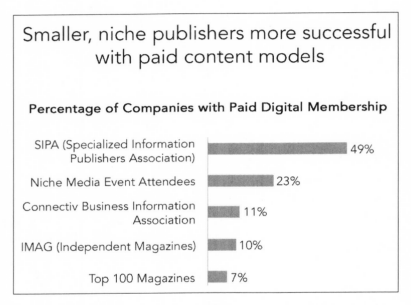

Smaller, niche publishers more successful with paid content models

Percentage of Companies with Paid Digital Membership

SIPA (Specialized Information Publishers Association) — 49%
Niche Media Event Attendees — 23%
Connectiv Business Information Association — 11%
IMAG (Independent Magazines) — 10%
Top 100 Magazines — 7%

While only 7 percent of the top 100 magazines earned money from a paywall or digital membership system, nearly half of specialized niche publishers did. Niche publishers have a track record of successful revenue generation by following this path. If you are a niche publisher and not charging for your content, it's time to start.

What Are People Afraid Of?

Despite this track record of success, many publishers are afraid to charge for access. I hear the same concerns over and over from my clients. Perhaps you're hitting one of these mental roadblocks right now yourself. We can debunk the myths underlying these fears:

1. *"No one will pay for my content."*
Publishers often fear competing against free content. They think, "My competitors are giving all this stuff away for free. There's no way I could charge for it."

To that I would reply—why are you in business? If you don't believe that your content is better than the competition's, then you need to find another way you can provide value. There is content people will pay for, and you can create it. You simply have to figure out your whales' unmet needs so you can create content that offers a solution. Or, if their needs are already met, you need to meet their needs better than your competitors do. This book will help you ask yourself the right questions and find the right angle to take with your content so that you can carve out a niche of paying customers.

2. *"If I give some of my content away for free, no one will pay for any of it."*
Successful publications have debunked this myth time and time again. Giving some of your content away for free is *essential* for driving awareness and interest in your membership products.

Different content serves different purposes. Some content is designed to pique interest, some is designed to solve a problem, etc. You simply have to understand what purpose each piece of content serves and place it on either side of your paywall accordingly. Then you can drive your warmest leads toward your paid content.

Why do some publishers fail to do so? Chiefly for two reasons:

- They don't apply best practices in content marketing to figure out what should be free and what should be paid, what people are willing to pay for, and what type of content drives engagement.
- They don't follow best practices in e-commerce sales and marketing concerning lead nurturing, asking for the sale, irresistible trial offers, etc.

If you put the right strategies in place (which you will learn how to do in this book), you can and *should* give away some of your content for free to generate leads, and then charge those leads for content that drives results.

3. Google will ding me.

Google has recently changed the rules of the game—again. Usually when people hear "Google has changed the rules of the game," it's cause for panic. "Oh no, will my traffic plummet because of an algorithm adjustment? Will the quality of my leads suffer?"

For once, however, Google has made a rule change that is *good* for content creators. Google will no longer ding you in search results for having quality content behind a paywall. That means you can create a membership model and still rank well in Google searches.

Which Numbers Are Important to Your Business?

Most publishers don't know how to shift to making money by charging for their content. Even publishers that do not rely on advertising still make tons of mistakes when selling their content online. Why?

Before you can make money online, you have to acquire a thorough understanding of your own business and your customers: Which numbers are important to your business? What business are you really in? Who are your whales?

Most publishers focus on engagement metrics—website traffic, Facebook fans, social media shares, etc. Measuring engagement is a vestige of the advertising model, because in the old days advertising revenue was based on the number of eyeballs you had—the number of people who bought your magazine, watched your TV show, listened to your radio show, or received a copy of your newsletter. It made sense to track those numbers because marketing was less sophisticated than it is now; the only metrics available were the number of people who saw the ad and the number of sales you had.

Today, more advanced metrics have made traffic measurement alone obsolete. There are better numbers out there for you to focus on to grow your business. The numbers that are important to your business are ones that will measure the engagement of *your key content consumers*. Five hundred engaged e-mail subscribers who read everything you send are more valuable than

50,000 people who signed up for e-mails after a contest and will never pay attention to you again.

Still, many publishers, even those that have started charging for their content, chase eyeballs instead of quality customers. When they fail, they blame the paywall, even though the problem was that they were focusing on the wrong numbers.

So how do you learn which numbers are important to your business? Well, first you have to discover what business you're really in, which will help you identify your key customers.

What Business Are You Really In?

There is a deeper answer to this question than "publisher" or "content creator." When I first talk to a publisher, I ask them, "What business are you in?"

They usually say, "I'm a publisher."

I'll reply, "But what business are you *really* in?"

They may get creative and say, "I'm in the content creation business."

That's a little better. Then I push: "No, what business are you *really*, **really** in?"

When we get down to it, the business they're really in is not always what they expect. Movie theaters, for example, aren't *really* in the entertainment business— they're actually in the restaurant business. Their goal is to get you to buy a Coke and some nachos, not a movie ticket.

According to *Business Insider*, "Movie theaters are not making money on movies, they are making money on food."[16] Movie theaters only keep around 30 percent or less of box office revenue; the studios keep the rest of it. So how do theaters make money? They make 85 percent of their profit on all concessions—which explains why a Coke costs $6. They're really in the food selling business.[17]

When I ask clients what business they're in, I'm looking for answers like, "I'm in the education business, which means I am in the business of teaching people something that they need to know, and making them better at it so that they can make more money, save more time, or be less stressed."

A clear answer includes who your target customer is and what problem you solve for them. For my client *Brew Your Own*, a publisher of content about homebrewing, the answer is, "We're in the business of teaching serious homebrewers how to become better at their craft."

There are many types of businesses you could be in as a niche publisher, and who your whales are depends on what business you're in.

---

[16] Myles Udland, "Here's How Movie Theaters Are Still Making Money Even Though Ticket Sales Are Down," *Business Insider*, February 18, 2015, http://www.businessinsider.com/movie-concessions-drive-amc-earnings-2015-2.
[17] Brad Tuttle, "Movie Theaters Make 85% Profit at Concession Stands," *Time*, December 7, 2009, http://business.time.com/2009/12/07/movie-theaters-make-85-profit-at-concession-stands/.

What Business Could You Be In? And Who Are Your Whales in Each One?

Education

What is it? Your content teaches customers how to solve a certain kind of problem. Publishers in the education business create quality "how-to" content.

Examples: Masterclass, *Fine Woodworking*, *Brew Your Own*, Athlean-X

Who are your whales? Consumers of your content

If your main goal is to educate, the most successful business model will likely be to create a paid membership for customers to access your content. Advertising is the cherry on top, but education businesses can survive on reader revenue alone if they strategize thoughtfully.

Fine Woodworking teaches you how to be a better woodworker. *Brew Your Own* teaches you how to be a better homebrewer. Athlean-X helps you get in shape with workout programs and meal plans exclusive to members of "Team Athlean." Masterclass offers courses delivered by A-listers in various fields, such as acting, writing, sports, etc. All these companies succeed by creating content that meets their customers' needs and creating a membership model to charge them for it.

Entertainment

What is it? Your content entertains.

Examples: Mobile gaming, HBO, *The Athletic*

Who are your whales? Consumers of your content

This one is simple: Companies charge their customers for entertainment. Mobile gaming companies charge either for the games themselves or for in-game purchases. Entertainment producers like HBO and *The Athletic* charge for access to entertaining content.

Information and Data

What is it? *Vital information, news, research, or statistics that serve a practical purpose.*

Examples: *The New York Times, the Boston Globe, Politico*

Who are your whales? *Consumers of your content*

News outlets have an opportunity to carve off niches and charge for access. Just as *Politico* created Politico Pro, the *Boston Globe* launched a healthcare industry niche membership product called "Stat." The *Globe* is still geared toward a mass audience and ad revenue, but they recognized a valuable niche of healthcare companies in Boston, created premium content for them, and charged them for access.

Lead Generation

What is it? You sell qualified leads to vendors.

Examples: Elderlawanswers.com and equippedbrewer.com

Who are your whales? Companies that purchase qualified leads from you (NOT the end consumer of your content)

Based on how visitors interact with your content, you can acquire data about who is in the market for a certain product or service in your industry. You then sell that information for a premium price to businesses in the form of qualified leads for them.

Elderlawanswers.com creates content about elder law, such as on what to do if your parents are going senile, or if you need to write a trust, etc. They have a list of lawyers on their site, and their hope is that you read their content and request more information by filling out a form. They then sell your name to a lawyer as a qualified lead.

The Equipped Brewer is an online publication dedicated to the success of young craft beverage companies. They generate leads for brewing equipment manufacturers by creating content for people who want to build brewing businesses; then they gather insight about qualified leads and pass that critical information on to equipment vendors.

This is very different from *Brew Your Own*, which is in the education business and charges homebrewers a membership fee to read great content. *The Equipped Brewer*'s revenue comes from the brewing equipment companies—their whales. The content still has to serve the readers' needs to get them to come to the site—which is what makes them qualified leads—but it also needs to drive qualified leads and filter out unqualified ones for their clients.

Marketing

What is it? Driving brand awareness for companies; you're essentially an offshoot of your clients' marketing agencies.

Examples: Good Housekeeping, Rachael Ray Every Day

Who are your whales? Advertisers, sponsors (NOT the end consumer of your content)

If you are in the business of getting people to identify with a brand, and you have amassed a loyal following of people in a specific "psychographic" or "demographic," you are probably in the branding business.

Advertising is a perfectly appropriate revenue stream in this business. You can use your brand halo to generate awareness for your sponsors, who are your whales. However, that doesn't mean you can simply rely on banner ads and pop-ups. You need to serve the needs of your whales (the advertisers) better than anyone else. You have to constantly ask yourself what you can do to help your advertisers build brand awareness with your like-minded audiences. Can you create sponsored events or special products? Custom publications? Custom content?

The *New York Times* delivered an effective advertising campaign for Netflix in which they published articles about real-life women's prisons.[18] They cobranded the articles with the Netflix show *Orange Is the New Black* (which is set in a women's prison), and informed readers that the show is "now streaming on Netflix." They created custom content that their audience would enjoy in order to promote the Netflix show, providing far more value to Netflix than a simple banner ad.

This practice, which is known as "native advertising," is not without its risks: By blurring the line between advertising and editorial content, the *Times* risked damage to its reputation—and therefore damage to its brand. Native advertising is certainly an improvement over the crass, transparent "advertorial" model that preceded it, but the *Times'* embrace of this practice has nevertheless earned it some public criticism from external sources—and even in

---

[18] *New York Times* paid post: https://paidpost.nytimes.com/netflix/women-inmates-separate-but-not-equal.html.

the paper's own pages. [19] Fortunately, the *Times'* subscribers—its whales—forgave it because the sponsored content was clearly labeled as such ... and because they consider the *New York Times* an indispensible part of their lives. This underscores what I said at the beginning of chapter 1: your reputation as a quality content provider is much more important than the money you earn from advertising.

Community Building

What is it? In the consumer world, it means you connect enthusiastic hobbyists and experts. In the B2B (business to business) world, it means you bring together all aspects of an industry: suppliers, customers, consultants, financiers, etc.

Examples: Melcrum, which offers a membership program and series of summits to foster a community for corporate communications professionals

Who are your whales? Consumers of your content, attendees at your events

Melcrum's whales are senior internal communications professionals at large companies. Melcrum provides them with a membership that includes shared cost research, advisory services,

---

[19] John Oliver, "Native Advertising," *Last Week Tonight,* August 3, 2014, https://www.youtube.com/watch?v=E_F5GxCwizc; David Carr, "Storytelling Ads May Be Journalism's New Peril," *New York Times,* September 15, 2013.

training, tools, and facilitated networking opportunities.

By building a deep connection through a community model, members are more willing to share their true, fundamental needs, which Melcrum can meet with better research, better tools, and better networking formats. This is a virtuous circle, leading to deeper connections and more honest sharing.

Research and Data

What is it? You sell research and data to companies or people that they can use to meet their goals (e.g., identifying the best growth opportunities for their businesses).

Examples: Healthcare Business International

Who are your whales? Businesses that purchase the reports (NOT the subjects of the reports)

The research and data business is a B2B model by nature. However, if you are a B2C publisher, you can still get into this game if you sell research about your audience—their habits, behaviors, and preferences—to vendors in your industry.

Healthcare Business International (HBI) uses independent, original news and analysis to provide a database of insights and comprehensive, structured coverage for the private healthcare industry. Their whales include VPs within big companies that have M&A (mergers and acquisitions) responsibility. HBI's database helps those VPs do their job—identify possible acquisition candidates that fit their investment thesis before anyone else swoops them up. Then HBI's hosted events allow the VPs to meet the CEOs of such companies and form relationships with them, which further helps the success rate of acquisitions.

•••

No matter what business you're in, you should apply the techniques in this book to your whales, whether they are end users, advertisers, or business partners. Find the best way to serve them, and relentlessly focus on meeting their needs. That's how you make money online today. By doing this you can reap amazing rewards, just as my clients have.

The Light at the End of the Tunnel

One publisher I worked with had suffered five straight years of decline before I got involved. I applied the principles in this book to their company, and in just three years we grew the top line by $20 million and the bottom line by 50 percent.

Because we put the right practices in place, that company is pretty much guaranteed to continue growing despite negative trends in the industry. We figured out which numbers actually matter to the business, and we watch those numbers *very* closely.

In the next chapter, I will outline the five forces of a successful strategy for making money online—the same five forces I used to take another company from zero to seven-figure digital business within one year. And yet another client applied these tools to achieve an immediate sixfold increase in digital revenues.

If you follow these strategies, you can set your content business on the path to sustained, double-digit revenue growth.

CHAPTER THREE

INTRODUCING THE FIVE FORCES

IN THIS CHAPTER, I'll introduce the five forces you can harness to maximize income from your whales. Each one has an entire chapter dedicated to it, but here's a brief summary of the overarching strategy needed to succeed online.

If you do it right, you can make a fortune. Remember the *Politico Pro* example from the last chapter? *Politico Pro* subscriptions start at $10,000 for individuals, and the publication is estimated to make over $100 million just from its membership subscriptions.[20] If you have the content and the community, as *Politico* does, the profit potential is there.

It's not as simple as erecting a paywall or finding a consultant to handle it for you. You could hire a marketing agency, but most of them are just trying to drive traffic to your website. They're not necessarily

---

[20] Max Willens, "How 4 of the Priciest Content Subscriptions Stack up," *Digiday*, August 10, 2017.

thinking about your goal: getting people to *pay for access to your content.*

Without a solid plan in place for content, audience development, and marketing, no matter whom you hire, and no matter what software you use, you aren't going to generate reader revenue.

However, by leveraging the five forces described in this book, you can create a powerful and profitable strategy for your business—a fast-growing audience that will line up to pay for your content is within reach. If you target those whales, figure out how to land them and keep them captive, and explore ways to expand your influence and value, your business will thrive.

Force #1: Focus on Your Whales

Your first priority should be finding your whales—your most engaged and enthusiastic customers. I've covered various businesses that have succeeded by focusing relentlessly on their whales: Dollar Shave Club, Wynn Resorts, and *The Athletic.*

To focus on your whales, you first have to understand them. Who are they? Where are they? What do they want? Are they coming to your website? Why or why not?

Answer these questions by talking to your whales, conducting surveys, and looking at behavioral studies. It's vital to discover the right way to talk to your whales to determine their underlying wants and needs. What value proposition will you offer your whales? What problem do you solve for them, and how? You can discover all of that by listening to them.

Force #2: Be Conversion-Oriented

You've identified your whales, you understand what they want, and you know what value you're offering them. How do you convert them into paying customers? Anyone can suggest a list of possible approaches. But after studying many of the companies succeeding in this space, I have determined that the top factor leading to conversions is how well you communicate your value proposition. People will not pay for something unless they understand and appreciate its worth.

I've personally witnessed the impact of clear value proposition communication on conversion, and extensive research has been done on this phenomenon. ConversionXL studied dozens of websites and found that a missing or poor value proposition was by far the most common factor limiting conversion rates.[21] The value proposition is "the #1 thing that determines whether people will bother reading more about your product or hit the back button."[22]

Mastery of this force boils down to giving enough away to your whales to demonstrate that value proposition—a taste, you might say—but nothing more. If your product worth is easy to describe and understand, you may only need good marketing copy

---

[21] Peep Laja, "What I Learned from Reviewing 45+ Websites (Are You Making the Same Mistakes?)," *ConversionXL*, last modified August 11, 2017, https://conversionxl.com/blog/what-i-learned-from-reviewing-websites/.
[22] Peep Laja, "Useful Value Proposition Examples (and How to Create a Good One)," *ConversionXL*, last modified August 11, 2017, https://conversionxl.com/blog/value-proposition-examples-how-to-create/.

to sell to your whales. If your product is more complex, or you're in a competitive business and it's tough to differentiate your product until the person actually lives and breathes what you have to offer, then you may want to explore free trials or guided demos. It all depends on what business you're in, whom you're targeting, and how hard it is to demonstrate your value proposition.

Force #3: Upsell

You're attracting and converting large numbers of whales into paying customers. At this point, many businesses want to move on to new customers—the fish. But you shouldn't stop focusing on your whales yet. Why? It's **five to seven times easier to sell to an existing customer than to find a new one**.

So, the question becomes: What else can you sell your whales? A lot of people don't have an upsell strategy because they don't think they have anything else to sell. It's time to build a **product pyramid**. You don't have to reinvent the wheel to come up with new products; you can repackage your existing content and assets into new, salable products. At each level of the pyramid you're solving the same problem for the same whales—you're just solving it at different levels.

Take my company as an example: the base of my product pyramid is my free blog, and low-cost items such as this book; the second tier is in-person workshops and training; the third is custom development of a digital marketing plan for your business, grounded in all five forces from this book; the fourth is all that *plus* ongoing coaching; and the fifth is a valet model—a company will hand over the keys to its website and say, "Make it work."

There are fewer customers at the top of the pyramid, but you're adding the most value there, and therefore charging the highest fee. At the bottom, you're still adding value—just less value for a lower price.

Force #4: Measure and Experiment

Leveraging Google Analytics, A/B split tests, data dashboards, and other metrics can help you maximize and optimize what you've built. We answer the questions "What should we measure?" and "How do we define success?" Course corrections may be necessary. When is it time to pull the plug on offerings that don't work, and what lessons can you learn?

I like to ask clients: What is our **learning agenda**? In other words, what would we like to discover about our customers that we should test? What's the right price? What's the right trial period? How do we best explain the value proposition? Which content should we give away to generate leads?

You should have a bunch of these open-ended questions. You don't have to answer them with your team—ask your customers! I've seen a lot of executive teams waste time debating these questions in a conference room when the only real way to answer them is to start testing with customers. In a later chapter we'll cover various experiments you should always be running and which metrics you should track.

Force #5: Create Bandwidth

The fifth force involves building a productive infrastructure to start executing. You may be thinking, "Hey, Rob, this all sounds great, but we don't have the time/people/resources!" My response would be that in today's environment, between software tools, freelancers, employees, agencies, and consultants, you can *find* the resources.

I will show you **how to create the bandwidth, find the right vendors, and effectively communicate what you need from them** now that you have a strategy. My company directly works with clients to help them build out the structures they need to implement all five of these forces.

These five forces aren't sequential. Ultimately, all five should be executed simultaneously and continuously to ensure sustained growth. Even the whale watching (Force 1) isn't a one-time thing. Your whales' wants and needs change. For example, they might age in or out. Many magazine publishers focus on subscribers who are sixty or seventy years old. Their whales are aging out. Other groups target millennials, who are now in their late thirties and have more money to spend. Those whales are aging in.

A good business strategy includes all five of the forces described in this chapter, and in the chapters that follow, we'll dive deep into each one. The first is "whale watching"—identifying your whales, determining their needs, and clarifying what you're offering them.

CHAPTER FOUR

FORCE #1:
FOCUS ON YOUR WHALES

FOCUSING ON YOUR whales means identifying your best customers and their needs. Traditional consumer research wisdom says to reach out to people who *don't* buy from you to figure out why not. While there's certainly some value to that, you can learn much more from the people who are most loyal to you—information that you can then use to find more customers like them.

It's important to distinguish between your whales and your biggest customers: Your whales are your most *enthusiastic* customers—not necessarily the highest-paying ones. There's a good chance that your whales *are* your highest-paying customers, but it's risky to assume so. You may have whales who aren't paying you much right now, but who love your product and *could* pay you more. Or you may have high-paying customers who are only subscribing to your content because the alternative is more expensive. They're not really whales, because as soon as a competitor's price drops, they'll leave. Their feedback is not that useful.

You should be looking for your most avid fans. True whales are thrilled about your product. They tell their friends about your content and encourage them to check it out, which creates a domino effect of similar whales finding your company.

The great thing about your whales is that *they are already captive.* You don't have to seek out people who are not your customers; your whales are surrounding your boat at this very moment. This strategy is built on leveraging your fan base. To maximize your revenue, you just need to identify who those fans are and what problems you're solving for them. This is easy to do— ask them.

Dan Oswald, CEO of Simplify Compliance, is a great example of someone who found his company's whales. He and his team found a niche to fill: professionals who code medical records for insurance companies. They discovered that this group was engaged but underserved. Theirs was an important and growing profession, but there was no agency, association, trade group, or publication targeted to them. So Simplify Compliance created the Association of Clinical Documentation Improvement Specialists (ACDIS)—a membership model. The mission of the ACDIS is "to serve as the premier healthcare community for clinical documentation specialists, providing a medium for education, professional growth, program recognition, and networking."[23] Members have access to peer-reviewed position papers and white papers, a bimonthly publication—the *CDI Journal*—and to job postings, among *numerous* other perks.

The ACDIS was a huge success, and these "whales" are now deeply engaged—members even show up to events dressed in the association's colors, orange and purple! They also have an e-commerce site where they sell ACDIS swag (pens, tote bags, etc.).

Find Your Whales, and Learn What Matters to Them

To properly monetize your whales, you need to offer a strong value proposition. The way to do that is to gather data from your whales to understand what they need. There are five steps to creating the right value proposition:

1. Identify your whales.
2. Interview five to seven whales.
3. Survey thirty to one hundred whales.
4. Create your value proposition.
5. Test your value proposition.

1. Identify Your Whales

Understanding your audience begins with recognizing that it consists of several sub-segments with different wants and needs. It makes sense to categorize your customers accordingly.

---

[23] "Mission Statement," ACDIS, accessed February 21, 2018, https://acdis.org/membership/mission.

Segmentation is vital if you want to grow, because it allows you to lower marketing costs while increasing sales. While some companies worry that focusing on a narrow slice of the market will limit sales, it actually does the opposite, enabling you to focus on many segments to grow your business. The key is specificity in whom you are targeting.

You don't need to hire a data science team to perform a cluster analysis to identify the customers who are most engaged with your brand (although if you can afford to, it may be worthwhile). There's still plenty you can do with a smaller budget. In fact, you can do quite a bit without spending a dime.

First, tap into your e-mail service provider's analytics. Most e-mail software offers "lead scoring," which provides insight into the expected value of each name on your e-mail list, allowing you to rank your leads. Find the 5 percent of your database with the highest score.

Second, you can complete an RFM (Recency, Frequency, Monetary) analysis in Excel. Track customers who have engaged **recently** and **frequently**, and have purchased within the past year.

Third, find people who have shared or commented on *at least three pieces of your content*, and cross-reference that list with your paid customers list. Don't focus on likes, because it's too easy to just "like" content. Remember, whales must have enthusiasm and commitment—they share or comment regularly.

Fourth, take a look at your Google Search Console to find out what search terms are bringing people to your site. You may find some surprises. One of my clients, a regional magazine, focuses on what most regional magazines highlight: local happenings, local politics, restaurants, entertainment venues, etc. Never had they published content about dating. But their Google Analytics revealed a surprising and valuable insight— the magazine attracted a lot of people seeking ideas for date spots. This led to a whole new product designed for single whales, and the idea to partner with online dating services.

You can also use qualitative sources to find your whales. Ask your content providers and sales team to identify passionate niche groups within your audience. The best groups are engaged but underserved, like the ACDIS members described earlier.

2. Talk to Five to Seven Whales

For each segment you identify, set up five to seven interviews with existing audience members. The goal of the interviews is to identify possible value propositions to test in a survey of a broader sample. Look for both technical and emotional elements of the value proposition.

Technical elements are things like how we can help our whales make more money, reduce costs, save time, or eliminate wasteful or annoying tasks.

Emotional elements include things like how we can entertain our whales, or help them feel more confident, get recognized or appreciated, connect with others, grow personally or professionally, or contribute to society.

To determine what these elements should be, ask the

following general questions (customize these questions to fit your brand):

- How did you get started in this field? Why is this category important to you?
- What do you care about when it comes to this category?
- What are the annoyances related to this field that you wish you could eliminate?
- How do our products meet your needs today? How do you use what we offer? (Ask about some of those technical elements mentioned earlier.)
- How do our products and services make you feel? (Ask about emotional elements.)
- How could we better meet your needs?
- What needs are we not meeting? Are there other companies that meet these needs for you?

You should also collect basic demographic information—age, gender, household income, etc.—if it's not already in your database. Once you've conducted all your interviews, summarize your key findings:

- What needs are consistently identified?
- How are those needs typically met today?
- What opportunities do you have to address those needs better?

- What emotional attributes are related to the category? (Look for common themes in answers to the question "How do these products make you feel?")

3. Survey Thirty to One Hundred Whales
Next, you should validate the results of your interviews by surveying at least thirty to one hundred whales. This will help you refine your value proposition. Here is a straightforward approach to creating an effective survey:

Based on the interview results, write fifteen to twenty statements about your whales' attitudes (their wants, needs, and general feelings about the category).

Using an online survey tool, ask your whales, "How strongly do you agree or disagree with each of the following statements?"

The survey statements cannot be generic; they must be tailored to what you learned in the interviews about your whales' wants and needs. They are different for every content provider. Later in this chapter I'll give you an example of the survey questions I came up with after I conducted my own whale interviews.

As you can see from these surveys, you should be very specific with statements that relate to your whales' wants and needs. Once you've gathered survey responses and analyzed them, you can then create a concise and powerful value proposition.

4. Construct Your Value Proposition

Publishers can achieve double-digit growth in conversion rates simply by better defining and communicating their value propositions. Your **value proposition** is a statement that clearly communicates who your target audience is, what needs they have, and how your product will meet those needs. Who are your whales? What problems do you solve for them? Why do these problems matter? When and where are they experiencing these problems? How do you solve these problems better than anyone else? If you can't answer **who**, **what**, **when**, **where**, **why**, and **how**, then you need to further develop your value proposition.

I recommend developing both a short and long version of a value proposition. The short version needs to be placed front and center on your home page, preferably next to a call to action (free trial, contact us, etc.). The long form—a longer description with more supporting material—is useful in other contexts.

To reiterate: it's important to tap into both physical and emotional attributes. People buy on emotions, then retroactively justify their decisions with facts. Make sure you understand how your product addresses at least one of the emotional drivers listed earlier in this chapter (the desire to feel confident, be entertained, get recognized or appreciated, connect with others, grow personally or professionally, or contribute to society).

For example, Unbounce, a company that helps marketers and digital agencies design landing pages and increase their website conversions, has a high-level value proposition on the top of their home page that connects to four emotional needs: confidence (you *will* build landing pages fast and increase conversions), recognition (you *will* become an awesome marketer), growth (you *will* increase conversion rates), and connection with others (join 14,000+ brands—including the *New York Times* and Vimeo).

This value proposition directly solves a problem that marketers face: How do I build landing pages and increase conversion rates?

Brew Your Own magazine's value proposition is "Brew like an expert: *Finally*, an online source of trusted information for homebrewers who like to make great beer." This addresses the human needs for certainty, significance, growth, and community.

The *New York Times* skillfully taps into its customers' need for **contribution**. They make their whales feel that by subscribing to the *Times*, they are fighting the good fight against clickbait and fake news.

The *Times* claims that by subscribing, you are supporting "truth," thereby *improving society as a whole*. Readers believe they're contributing not just to the *Times*, but to the world. That's a powerful emotional motivator.

Case Study: Sterling Woods Group

Let's bring this chapter to life with an example. When I started my business, I interviewed a bunch of whales— owners and senior executives of media companies. Here is a summary of my interview notes on what they told me:

Tangible needs that currently are not satisfactorily met:
- **Make more money:** I need to monetize what I'm doing online. Digital ad dollars are small and declining. My online activities help with soft things like "engagement" but I have not been able to turn that "engagement" into money.
- **Save costs:** I know I need to do more online, but don't have a ton of cash to invest. How can I reduce the amount of investment I need to shift more of my revenue to digital sources?
- **Save time:** I'm tired of working hard chasing every new shiny object: Pinterest, Snapchat, Instagram, etc. I just need to know what works and what does not, so I can focus on a small number of high-ROI initiatives instead of burning out by doing a little bit of everything.

Emotional needs:
- **Certainty:** The industry is in a state of flux and we need some stability. We don't have a large margin of error to play with. Whatever we do needs to work.

- **Connection:** We would like to see what other publishers are doing that works and share best practices with like-minded professionals.
- **Growth:** We "don't know what we don't know" about the digital world. Please help us understand it better.
- **Contribution:** We care about our audience. We want to use our journalism to further the interests of our niche.

Based on these notes, I sent out this survey to a broader set of whales:

On a scale of 1–7, how strongly do you agree with each of these statements? (1 = completely disagree, 4 = neutral, 7 = strongly agree)

❏ I am satisfied with the amount of revenue that comes from digital sources.

❏ My digital ad revenues are healthy and growing.

❏ I have a hard time converting online engagement (traffic, clicks, page views) into actual sales.

❏ I have sufficient capital to invest in digital growth initiatives.

❏ I feel a duty to serve my audience with the best journalism possible.

❏ I feel like I'm fighting fires all day.

❏ I understand which digital opportunities have the highest ROI for my business.

❏ My job or business would be at risk if I made one costly mistake.

❏ It's important for me to know what other similar publishers are doing to grow their digital revenues.

❏ I like networking with other publishers to share best practices.

❏ I wish I had a deeper understanding of the digital world.

❏ I know what types of content my readers would be willing to pay for.

Based on what surveyed well, I developed the following value proposition:

Short: "Make more money online: Proven marketing solutions for content creators—backed by results."

Long: "We work with niche publishers to unleash their profound (but hidden) market strengths and rich content archives to lock in growth of 50 percent or more. We've developed a series of five proven strategies that refocus a publisher's website and marketing efforts to systematically boost sales and profits. Publishers who embark on this growth path also find it *liberating*, because often, for the first time in years, they feel truly focused."

We focus on our whales' need for certainty. In the research, publishers told us that they are anxious about their futures. Many of our customers are longtime owners of their publications, and they're worried that they may not be in business much longer. We offer them certainty—*proven solutions backed by results.*

Our whales also told us that they feel like their companies are their babies, and they want to keep growing their businesses. Therefore, our value proposition also reflects the need for growth. We teach our clients five strategies to make more money online, so that they can apply them to their businesses and achieve the growth they *need.*

What counts as a value proposition? I tell my clients, "If you can think like a journalist, then you can easily develop a value proposition." Remember, all you have to know is the **who, what, why, when, where,** and **how**.

Again, you must know **whom** you're targeting. You know **what** problem you're solving for them. You know **why** this problem is meaningful to them. You know **when** and **where** they're experiencing this problem. And you know **how** you're going to solve this problem for them better than anyone else. If you can answer all those questions, then you have your value proposition.

Here are a few examples from our clients (with details altered somewhat for confidentiality purposes), including the original value propositions they gave me when I asked them in our kickoff session and the new value propositions we developed with them:

Company: A B2B publisher focused on the high-end home design market

Old value proposition: "We publish a high-quality weekly e-mail newsletter for the trade informing them of relevant local events and happenings."

New and improved value proposition: "Our membership helps independent design professionals find new clients that they are passionate about serving."

Company: A B2B magazine in the dairy industry

Old value proposition: "We have the most in-depth content on the dairy industry."

New and improved value proposition: "All the Industry's Buzz in One Spot:

Our members stay ahead of the competition because they get centralized access to practical news, consumer insights, and pricing trends across the *entire* industry."

Company: An organization that holds events for the healthcare industry

Old value proposition: "We put on high quality events for everyone in the industry."

New and improved value proposition: "We uncover hidden business development opportunities for member healthcare executives and help them network to increase customer acquisition."

5. Test Your Value Proposition

The goal of the value proposition is to drive conversions—i.e., to get your customers to sign up for an e-mail list, ask for a demo, enroll in a free trial, and of course, buy from you. You should constantly A/B test your value propositions to find the one that optimizes conversions. Then, every six months, you should re-assess your value proposition to make sure it remains valid.

Once you've created and optimized your value proposition, you can use it to drive conversions. Which brings us to the next chapter: How do you actually sell to your whales?

CHAPTER FIVE

FORCE #2:
BE CONVERSION-ORIENTED

THIS CHAPTER IS all about—you guessed it—**conversion**. Conversion means getting visitors to your site to perform a desired action, such as giving you an e-mail address, filling out a lead form—or, of course, buying something from you!

Conversion is often the largest immediate opportunity for content creators to improve. Why? Most media websites are focused on eyeballs, because under the advertising model, publishers get paid every time someone clicks on *anything*. It doesn't matter *what* the visitor clicks on—as long as a click gets registered, page views go up, and the publisher earns another fraction of a penny.

As a result of this dynamic, most media websites look ... hmm, how do I say this nicely ... terrible! There is too much stuff on each page, dizzying amounts of articles to click on, pop-up ads on top of pop-up ads (this isn't hyperbole—I've actually seen a pop-up ad literally *pop up over another pop-up*), videos that autoplay, and so forth.

If you follow the principles outlined in this chapter, you can quickly redesign your online experience to make it more conversion oriented, and reap the benefits. Now that you've identified your whales, their wants and needs, and what problem you're solving for them, you can focus on the key conversion question: *How do you actually sell to them?*

The process of turning existing traffic into paying customers is a three-part cycle:

1. Demonstrate value
2. Ask for the e-mail
3. Show, don't tell—with a risk-free offer

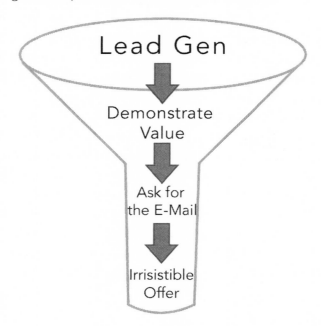

All my clients have achieved spectacular results following this conversion cycle, such as an eightfold increase in e-mail list size, a fivefold increase in trials, and a 50 percent increase in landing page conversion rate.

Let's walk through the cycle.

Demonstrating value requires placing some really good content in front of your paywall to attract customers. It all comes back to the value proposition—and you need to bring that promise to life. Typically, you'll use around 20 percent of your total content for lead generation. This content should be search-engine optimized and very relevant to your whales, and it should give your whales a sense of what they'll experience if they purchase your products. Yes, you *do* have to give away something valuable before you ask for an e-mail.

Your free content cannot be throwaway content, or clickbait like "Five Ways to Save a Dollar." It must be *high-quality content that demonstrates your value proposition* by demonstrating the benefits they'll receive from your membership program.

For example, the TV network Showtime gives away the first episode of every new series for free by posting it on YouTube. That's how they demonstrate their value: They provide a taste of the high-quality content you'd get as a subscriber. This gives their whales an opportunity to help market them, too; viewers generate positive word of mouth: "The first episode's free on YouTube" is information regularly shared among friends and co-workers, and it piques people's interest.

Not sure what to give away for free? A good place to start is looking at your Google Analytics to figure out which pieces of content are your star attractions (don't worry if this is too technical for you right now, I'll explain how best to use Google Analytics in chapter 7). What are people coming to your site for? It's best to keep that content free so you continue to attract traffic, which you can then move through your conversion funnel.

Ask for the e-mail: After your whales benefit from your free content, you can ask for their e-mail addresses. The best method for capturing e-mail addresses changes over time and varies from publisher to publisher depending on their whales' needs. However, there are a few universal rules that seem to work:

1. Not a lot of people want to sign up for yet another "free newsletter." Can you provide a more creative offering? For example, bundle the newsletter with a free white paper, download, coupon, video, etc.?

2. Test different freebies. Testing gives you more data to better understand your whales. For example, if you're an outdoor magazine, you can offer a guide on hiking gear, then one on camping gear, and then one on mountain-climbing gear. Based on the response you get, you learn more about who is coming to your site and what really matters to them.

3. In your "call to action" be sure to let your whales know how the free offer you're giving them in exchange for their e-mail addresses will solve a known problem for them. For example, instead of "Sign up for our CFO newsletter" use a call to action like "avoid costly and embarrassing mistakes by enrolling in our FREE weekly compliance alert."

Show, don't tell, with an irresistible, risk-free offer. After you've established your value and captured an e-mail address, you can make your prospect a "risk-free offer," so that you can nurture the lead by showing, not telling your value proposition, giving them a sample of the experience they can expect if they subscribe.

You have to find the balance between giving them something so that they want to pay for more—and not giving them *too* much so they feel they don't need to pay at all. The goal is to provide *just* enough to convince them to pay you.

So what does that mean for your business? It's different for every content creator. It can be as simple as having one amazing article that drives readers to buy from you. You're pretty lucky if that's all it takes—but sometimes it is. In that scenario, in order to convert your whales, all you'd have to do is give away that article for free and then ask for the sale.

But for many businesses it takes more than that, so there are various methods you can use to execute this step, which we'll outline below. Before settling on one or the other, it is important to understand the purpose behind the irresistible offer: to reduce a customer's perceived sense of risk.

What Is the Goal of an Irresistible Offer?

You need an irresistible offer to reduce customers' risk and make them feel comfortable purchasing. Showtime has a cancel-anytime policy, so no one feels locked in to a contract; there's no risk. Some companies offer a cash-back guarantee: "If you're not satisfied within 90 days, return your purchase and receive a full refund."

Some companies even offer *risk reversal*, which means that if customers don't like their product or service, they will not only provide a refund, but they'll give them something too. For example, Real Estate Exam Tutor, an educational website designed to help users prepare for the real estate exam, promises "110% satisfaction guaranteed": if, after using their system, you don't pass the exam, they'll refund 110% of your money.[24]

You can't lose by making a risk reversal offer: few people will take you up on it, and any losses incurred by those who do will be offset by the additional sales you'll make with that guarantee.

If you believe your content is worth the cost of your subscription fee, you should put your money where your mouth is. Make your audience an irresistible offer—a money-back guarantee, a cancel-anytime offer,

---

[24] "Guarantee," Real Estate Exam Tutor, accessed February 19, 2018, http://www.realestateexamtutor.com/Guarantee.

or a risk-reversal offer—that conveys your confidence that they'll be happy with it. That confidence greatly reduces customers' sense of risk.

If you're nervous about making an irresistible offer—if you're afraid of giving something away—then that's a good indication that you need to spend more time listening to your whales and defining a value proposition that addresses their needs. Once you have the right value proposition locked in, the question becomes, what's the right offer for your business?

Risk-Free Offer Options

So, what kind of offers are there, and which is right for you? Below are eight types of irresistible offers and the benefits and downsides of each.

1. Free Trial, No Credit Card Required
Prospects can sign up for free access to a product for a limited amount of time. The great thing about free trials that don't require a credit card is they streamline your sign-up process. The downside is you'll need a sales rep or marketing campaign to convert them into paying customers after their trial expires—or your leads will go cold quickly.

You also need to make sure the trial period is long enough for a customer to understand your value proposition. If it takes several weeks to really understand the power of your product, and you offer a five-day trial, few customers will pay up. Additionally, you should always couple a free trial with an **onboarding campaign**—a series of e-mails that encourage users to try different features of the product. This way, you nudge them toward understanding the benefits you offer.

2. Free Trial, Credit Card Required
Free trials with a credit card usually involve an automatic upgrade to a paid plan. The upside is that this model essentially automates the conversion process for you. The onus is on the prospect to cancel if they don't want to be rolled over into a paying subscription.

Amazon Prime is a classic example of this model. So is Showtime; Showtime offers a free, week-long trial of their entire platform (credit card required). That gives customers a chance to see if they like more than just the free episodes they've already watched on YouTube. If they want to subscribe, all they have to do is not cancel after the trial expires.

As with a free trial with no credit card required, you also need to make sure the trial period is long enough to demonstrate your value, and you need to support it with an onboarding campaign.

There are two major drawbacks to this model:
• Asking for a credit card can scare off prospects early in the process.
• You run a risk of boosted refunds. How

many times have we all realized we forgot to cancel a free trial only after it showed up on our monthly statement?

3. Free Trial, Credit Card Extension
This means you first give customers a free trial with no credit card required, and then, if the customer wants, they can extend their free trial in exchange for their credit card number.

Appcues offers its customers a two-week free trial with no credit card required. However, if prospects feel they need a little more time to decide whether to use the paid product, they can extend the free trial for five days in exchange for their credit card information. This offer has yielded stellar results: 66 percent of those who extend their trial convert to paid customers.

This model nicely combines the first two risk-free offers.

4. Freemium
A freemium model means offering a free version of a premium product. A good example is Candy Crush, a free mobile game with optional in-app purchases. You can play the entire game for free forever, but there are options to boost your experience if you're willing to pay. Another example is the cloud service Dropbox, which offers everyone a limited amount of free storage, but charges for larger storage capacity.

In the digital content area, you could follow this model by making some content free (like news or entry-level information) while gating off premium content (like how-to articles or advanced analysis). *Subscription Insider* does just that: news and features are always free, but how-to and best-practice articles are locked behind a paywall.

Critics of the freemium model argue it's not scalable in its classic form. The companies who see the most success have huge user bases and are backed by heavy-hitting investors.

5. Finite Free Content in Front of a Paywall ("Metered Paywall")

This model affords users a limited number of free clicks or visits and then blocks further access until they subscribe. Many major newspapers handle their digital content this way, such as the *New York Times*, which allows visitors to read five free articles per month. After that, the site blocks users from reading more until the month rolls over or they purchase a subscription.

This is a standout trial model for many publishers, which is why so many industry top dogs use it. It's a quick and easy way to display your value proposition while protecting some of your strongest assets.

But this model is most effective if your company produces a lot of high-demand content. If you don't publish new work very often, or if similar work can be found elsewhere for free, you'll have a hard time convincing readers they need to pay to access more of your content.

6. Free Demo

A free demo means that a sales professional offers a walk-through of the service or product. Demos work best with highly customizable or complex products and services, such as Politico Pro. If your content model is easy to understand ("For $50 per month, receive exclusive industry research reports in your inbox!"), then a demo won't be an effective value demonstration for your prospective customers.

But if your content service is a little more complex, with varying features that may appeal to some consumers and need some explaining, then a demo can educate your prospects on the amazing advantages your product offers.

7. Money-Back Guarantee

Money-back guarantees reduce risk by making it easy to cancel a service if the customer isn't happy. *Business Insider* has made smart use of this model. A money-back guarantee may be harder to sell upfront than a free trial, but if you're confident in the quality of your content, it provides a safety net for new members while still bringing in revenue for your business. You may also want to consider the risk reversal idea (110% money back) described above.

8. Free in Exchange for Promotion

You provide free access to your content in exchange for a customer marketing your product to others. For example, you can offer three months of access if a reader shares a referral link on Twitter and Facebook. The "unsubscription" service Unroll.me takes advantage of this model: When you launch the service for the first time, you can unsubscribe to e-mail lists. But after you unsubscribe to a certain number of lists, you have to stop for the day—*or* you can share the service on social media to "unlock" more features. This model doesn't necessarily result in direct revenue, but it can drive word-of-mouth advertising to boost your lead generation efforts.

Which One Is Right for You? Set Goals and Test Offers to Find Out

To find out which offer to provide your whales, consider the factors that are unique to your audience: What is the value of your content relative to their budget? How often do readers consume your content? If it's once a month, "10 free articles a month" isn't going to be an offer that drives conversion. How much exposure to your content do they need to make a buying decision?

Content creators need to constantly reevaluate the balance between offering free content to attract users and charging for content to protect their business model. You need to vary your marketing messages and digital user experience to appeal to each of your consumer segments. And you need to test, test, test.

For example, we might set an objective of converting the 2 percent of traffic that reads an article into paid customers. If we fall short of our goal, we analyze and modify our site to improve our conversion rate. Perhaps we improve the communication of our value proposition, or simplify the checkout process, or examine which type of irresistible offer we're using. We then use the results to guide the changes we make to our user experience, then re-run the experiment and remeasure the results. (I'll go into greater detail on tests and experiments in chapter 7.)

Converting your whales from nonpaying consumers into paying customers is the obvious first opportunity to monetize them. However, beyond conversion lies an even greater source of revenue and growth for your company: selling even more, higher-margin products to the whales you've just converted.

CHAPTER SIX

FORCE #3:
UPSELL

YOU HAVE A successful membership program in place ... but why stop there? You'd be leaving money on the table! Why not look for other products and services to sell your whales? Or what about products that you can sell your "fish" with the hope of transforming them into members over time?

Enter the product pyramid—a portfolio of different products and services at different price points and margins. The pyramid works because it's easier to upsell an existing customer with a new product than it is to find a new customer. People buy based on trust, so if they already have a good relationship with you, they are primed for the next purchase. Consider the following statistics:

- The average conversion for a first-time purchaser is just 5–20 percent, while upsell offers convert at 60–70 percent.[25]
- The average new e-commerce customer spends just $24.50, while the repeat customer spends more than double that— $52.50.[26]
- It costs six to seven times as much to acquire a customer as to retain or upsell them.[27]

On the following page is a sample product pyramid structure that works for many content creators. Product pyramids start with a lower-priced (or free) product aimed at the largest audience, and move up through premium, more expensive (and profitable) offerings directed at smaller segments of your audience. The main purpose of this pyramid is get your whales on board at a relatively low price point, then retain and upsell them over time. The right progression of products should be tailored to meet your whales' needs and capitalize on the relationships you build with them.

---

[25] Paul W. Farris et al., *Marketing Metrics*, 2nd ed. (Saddle River, NJ: Pearson FT Press, 2010).

[26] Michael Fung, "Top 6 Statistics That Should Change How You Use Marketing Automation to Increase Sales," Marketing Is Sales, January 18, 2014, accessed February 21, 2018, http://www.marketingissales.com/top-6-statistics-that-should-change-how-you-use-marketing-automation-to-increase-sales/.

[27] Ibid.

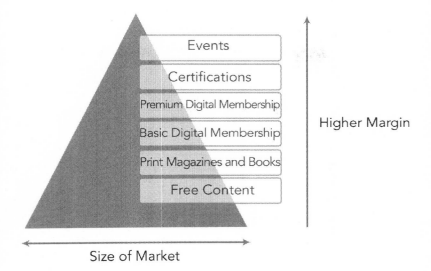

Why Build a Pyramid?

Primary opportunity: high margins at the **top of the pyramid!** If you don't have an attractive, high-margin offering at the top of your pyramid, you should rework your business model to accommodate one. Usually at the top of the pyramid are items such as events, associations, mastermind groups, consulting, training, certifications, custom research, or databases. The price point should be at least hundreds of dollars if you are a consumer brand, or thousands of dollars if you are B2B. All of these items should be tailored around your content. For example, perhaps you could offer custom research that goes deeper into one of your content verticals. Or you could have an event that explores a key pillar of your editorial agenda. I'll get into more examples in a minute.

Secondary opportunity: **smaller commitments at the bottom of the pyramid.** At the base of the pyramid, you might consider a more affordable option to bring in some fish with the hopes of turning them into baby whales. Once you have built trust with those new customers you can funnel them upward toward your higher-priced product. Why not hold a regional event for $500 with the hopes of getting people to attend your national event for $3,000? The Content Marketing Institute does a fine job executing this strategy.[28]

The system should work as a whole, even if margins are slim to none at the bottom of the pyramid. It's okay to have near-zero margins on entry-level offerings so long as you demonstrate the ability to upsell your customers over time. However, I rarely advocate "loss leaders"—selling products at an explicit loss (except the "free" content you give away to build trust with your audience)—unless you can prove the investment pays for itself within twelve months.

Where Do I Start?

The answer is simple: **repurpose existing content**. Developing products to sell to existing customers doesn't necessarily involve creating a bunch of new content. You already have an archive of material that holds substantial value for your audience; one way to create new products is to put it into a new context.

The most basic form of repurposing content is a book publisher releasing a hardcover and then a

[28] Content Marketing Institute, http://contentmarketinginstitute.com/about/.

paperback edition of the same book. Movies are released in theaters, then on DVD and to streaming services, then on television. This concept of repackaging means changing the context, the format, the pricing, and the target audience.

Products and services should be built around your **evergreen content**—material that stands the test of time. You will likely need to massage it a little to align it with your value proposition, but you should develop products that are largely based on repurposed content.

What Should Go Toward the Top of the Pyramid?

Research has shown that consumers are more willing to pay for certain types of content. Make sure these conditions are met as you move up the pyramid, so that you have higher-margin offerings to upsell your whales into:

- Content that supports a job or career (e.g., premium memberships like Business Insider or Statista). Think: Can they write it off? Can they use it to advance their careers?

- Material that helps enthusiasts invest and improve skills in their hobbies or offers the ability to interact with other like-minded professionals or hobbyists.

- Content with high entertainment value (e.g., blockbuster games, music, and films).

- Content that adds value through the user experience (e.g., instead of a PDF version of a magazine archive, a searchable, interactive repository with intelligent recommendations).

Here are some specific digital product ideas that fit one or more of the above criteria—and have proven successful for content creators.

Certifications

Content businesses are uniquely positioned to tap into this market: They already possess the resources and authority to produce high-value learning and certification products. Consumers are more likely to pay for content if they believe they are getting a specific benefit from it (i.e., a particular skill, an insider's knowledge, or special recognition).

If you are in a competitive space, you will need to find an advantage, something that separates you from the pack. You might use your authority or status in the market to create some sort of certification. Many publishers and content creators have found success by offering a certification process and putting courses behind a paywall (of course, this must be content that people cannot get for free on YouTube):

- **Content Marketing Institute**, which offers free daily e-newsletters, also operates Content Marketing University (http://www.contentmarketinguniversity.com), a series of online marketing courses, with annual fees ranging from $595 to $995 ("alumni" get a break on pricing).

The newsletters drive registrations for the university, as well as for Content Marketing World and other lucrative live events.

- **TrackMan** produces golf radar equipment. They're a fun company— I've worked with them. We developed TrackMan University (http:// trackmanuniversity.com), which offers free content in addition to golf instructor certification material—the latter for a $475 annual fee. TrackMan University's tools give instructors the opportunity to learn valuable skills to make them better teachers, and a certification they can use in their marketing materials.

Another advantage you can promote is the fact that your reach within the community will allow students to network with one another. The public speaking organization Toastmasters follows this approach. Members can progress through levels of the program and earn recognition and credentials along the way, from the first-tier awards of "Competent Communicator" and "Competent Leader" all the way through the "Accredited Speaker Program" for professional speakers. It all comes back to gamification and getting people connected to the brand.

Don't forget that you likely have content that can be repurposed for online certification courses. Naturally, you will need to piece it together, and perhaps create some supplemental material, such as videos, exercises, and quizzes. When developing certification materials, you should be filling the gaps in existing content rather than starting from scratch.

Selling Data

You collect a lot of digital information about your audience that has commercial value to other businesses. Say you publish a regional e-magazine targeted at high net-worth individuals in your area. You can track their behavior (e.g., which e-mails they open, which articles they read) to predict who is likely to be in the market for a high-ticket item such as a new home, car, or financial advisor. You can then sell these leads for a premium to realtors, auto dealers, and financial services firms. You are doing your readers a favor by helping them make an important decision. Just be sure to properly disclose how you are using data.

You also may be able to provide useful data to help businesses with their marketing, sales, and forecasting needs. My favorite use of data from a content company is the Weather Channel's partnership with Wal-Mart: The latter uses the former's data to forecast sales. Looks like it's going to be rainy in Philadelphia? Better stock more umbrellas at Wal-Marts in the greater Philly area.

You can also repackage your reports, fact books, and databases and sell them to data-hungry businesses. For example, I've collected a lot of data about what percentage of companies use paywalls, the most common calls to action, and the most common business models. I can sell research reports on these subjects to my clients.

Many other companies offer compensation guides revealing what executives in a particular industry earn; or market share guides that identify the top players in a specific field; or contact directories, like a list of all the vice presidents of purchasing in an industry. You're probably sitting on the makings of a guide, database, fact book, white paper, or dossier that you can easily sell for premium bucks.

When it comes to potential buyers for your data, think beyond your typical audience. This information has value for consulting firms, investors, banks, insurance companies, lawyers, and other professional services that cater to your whales. These potential buyers also tend to have deeper pockets to pay for research.

The focal point of the pyramid should be your whales, but other people are also trying to get the attention of your whales, and you should be developing products with them in mind, too.

Events

If you've done a great job building community and trust, events are a prime way to monetize your content. Events should be near the top of your pyramid. These could be a combination of online webinars and in-person meetings, conferences, seminars, and so forth. They provide significant value to your whales and significant profit potential for you.

Some publishers worry that events aren't feasible because of logistical challenges. "I'm not an event planner" is a common thought for publishers. The good news is that there are many excellent third-party event planners. Sacrifice some margin in the short term and outsource the logistics. Once you get the hang of it you can always bring event management in-house, but to start you should leverage an event planner's expertise rather than driving your team crazy. Keep your team focused on what they do best, and find someone who can handle organizing and managing your event.

Events should be designed around the needs of your whales, and you should develop a list of potential attendees. You can test demand easily before you make a financial commitment to a venue—survey your whales: "We're having this event; how interested are you in registering presale?" If nobody bites, you can always cancel the event at no cost and consider an alternative.

TrackMan, the golf radar company mentioned above, has events centered around training and camaraderie. All TrackMan-certified instructors are invited to a couple of events throughout the year. Attendees can bring their equipment to have it tuned up by technicians; there are sessions describing how golf clubs and instructors are using TrackMan in novel ways to drive sales, and there are opportunities to mingle and share best practices.

I'd be hard pressed to find a publisher that should never consider events. If you're a niche publisher with a loyal following, you probably have readers who would love to meet your editorial staff and other subscribers.

Brew Your Own magazine hosts boot camps, bringing in prominent brewers to teach attendees new techniques. Entertainment publishers can put on a Comic-Con-style event for their niche.

This isn't to say your events have to be huge. You can start small and still do very well. Could you get ten of your most important readers to pay $1,000 a head for an executive summit or workshop? That's $10,000 for one day of your time.

What Goes on the Bottom of the Pyramid?

Free Stuff

Much has been written about "content marketing"— things you can give away for free to build your audience. Typical giveaways are things like white papers, guides, free downloads, free newsletters, free webinars, etc. Remember, as discussed in chapter 5, free stuff is an important element in conversion: you need to demonstrate your value proposition by giving away about 20 percent of your content for free.

Your Print Products

There may be an opportunity, if you don't already do so, to repurpose some of your print archives as special editions. If you're looking for a level of content for the bottom of your pyramid that's above free but below an annual subscription, you may be able to create some ad hoc print products by repurposing your archives. If you're a wine magazine, for example, you can publish a special "Best Cabernets" issue, or even a book—something like *100 of Our Favorite Merlots.*

E-Commerce

Marketers across industries spend more than $40 billion per year on content marketing—using valuable information to attract and convert customers. You have content! You have an audience that you know is passionate about a certain category! Why not use the content marketing model in reverse and sell products related to your category?

There are two flavors of e-commerce to consider. The first is selling products related to your brand (or as I like to say, the tchotchke business). Many people think, why don't we just add a store to our website? We can have our advertisers sell their stuff, and we can sell stuff, too. The problem is that people come to your website to consume content, not to buy anything; they go to Amazon to buy.

Amazon represents nearly half of US e-commerce sales.[29] **Don't try to compete with Amazon.** Few content businesses have done so and made real money. Of all the things you could do online, this will not provide the biggest bang for your buck.

A second, more profitable model is to embed

---

[29] Rani Molla, "Amazon Could Be Responsible for Nearly Half of US E-Commerce Sales in 2017," *recode*, October 24, 2017, https://www.recode.net/2017/10/24/16534100/amazon-market-share-ebay-walmart-apple-ecommerce-sales-2017.

affiliated marketing offers into your content. People rely on you for content, so why not present them with related products within that context? For example, if you have an article about camping that recommends a specific canteen, why not put a link to that canteen within the article? People will want to buy the canteen you're talking about because they trust your information. Your visitors will appreciate you saving them the hassle of figuring out where to buy the product: They know they're getting exactly what you recommended, and they don't need to leave your website to find it. You're helping the retailer by giving them a lead, and you're helping yourself because you can charge a commission on the sale or on the lead.

Don't expect affiliates to be a major revenue stream, however. Look at it as an effective way to improve your user experience and make some additional revenue from existing traffic without much work on your part.

A third, even more profitable model that *could* be more lucrative would be to sell high-ticket items related to your niche and work out favorable deals directly with the manufacturers or providers of these services. While you might be able to earn a 1–10 percent commission as an affiliate marketer, you could realize a 20 or maybe even 30 percent commission on high-end products if you qualify your audience members and turn them into buyers for your business partners.

The Building Blocks of Your Pyramid

Your pyramid has many optional components. How you should build your pyramid boils down to two factors: what business you are in, and who your whales are. Which products would best reflect your value proposition?

Once you hone in on your value proposition, you can pitch different concepts to your whales. Let's use the healthcare niche as an example. If we could bring together peers from many leading hospitals once a year, many of those potential attendees would find such a gathering extremely compelling. The freedom to compare notes without vendors or consultants trying to sell them anything would be invaluable.

Let your whales help you: Before you launch a new product, poll your whales to see if you can sell it to them. In the healthcare example, we might call the CEOs and say, "We understand that many CEOs would like the chance to network with their peers in a closed, structured format, without commercial distraction from vendors. Do you think this is a good idea? Great! We want to try it. We plan on charging $50,000 for future events, but for this first one, we plan to charge a nominal fee of $5,000. Would you like to register?"

For a less expensive product like a newsletter, we could say, "We're thinking about creating this newsletter. Would you be interested in receiving it on a trial basis? We'd like to hear what you think."

Getting your whales involved in product development and piloting new products is a way to obtain early feedback that will allow you to correct course before you spend a lot of money on a full-blown launch.

I like to survey customers and ask what they think of a few different ideas. If they rate something very highly, then I'll ask if they'd like to be a pilot customer for free or for a discount. This can help make sure there is an audience and build a base of potential buyers before you launch.

Look for what appeals to your whales to determine which of these products will best meet their needs.

Moving Your Customers up the Pyramid

Once you have a slate of new offerings in your product pyramid, you need a way to upsell. View the pyramid as a path upward for your customers. Make any initial barriers to the first purchase relatively low—wow them and give them what they want at that level. Then you'll see them move up the pyramid. It takes some patience, but if you stay disciplined, it will pay off. Customers are unlikely to take the leap directly from free to premium products.

The key to moving people up the pyramid is collecting data from them and targeting them with relevant e-mail marketing offers based on that data. You should be capturing e-mails for everyone, segmenting your e-mail list, and customizing your messages.

An e-mail list requires you to spend a bit of political capital. The tacit agreement when someone signs up is that in exchange for free content they will occasionally receive a sales pitch. Give away enormous value before asking for anyone's money. If an e-mail subscriber is on the verge of being interested in your brand and you invite them to join your exclusive council for $50,000 a year, you've squandered your political capital. Instead, you might start by offering a $20 webinar. Once they buy that, you can try to sell them a $200 annual newsletter subscription. If they bite, you can target them for a $2,000 event, and so forth. That's how you move people up the pyramid.

Technology can automate the process for you. If you've never done something like this before, start with a simple system. You can do a lot with inexpensive tools like MailChimp. Once you get the hang of segmentation and customizing offers, then you can graduate to middle-tier options like HubSpot, which combines e-mail with website visitor behavior. Then you can graduate to more sophisticated software that monitors people across all platforms.

Surveying your whales and offering them the opportunity to be pilot customers is an effective way to move them up the pyramid as well, because you can offer them a discount at first, then renew them at full price.

Metrics: How Do I Know I'm on the Right Track?

It's easy enough to determine whether your product pyramid approach is working. Measure your conversion rate from one level of the pyramid to the next. The conversion rate should increase as you rise through the pyramid. For example, using the sample pyramid above, while only 10 percent might convert from free content to a magazine subscription, you'd want to see more than 10 percent of magazine subscribers convert to a basic digital membership. If 20 percent of magazine subscribers choose the basic digital membership, then ideally more than 20 percent of those customers would upgrade to the premium digital membership.

If the conversion rate drops as you move up the pyramid, you have identified a bottleneck. Investigate to see if your product, price, and marketing message are on track. Or consider adding in another layer to bridge the two tiers—perhaps it's too large a leap from one side of that bottleneck to the other.

Measuring and optimizing your results is key to your growth. We'll explore ways to manage those processes in the next chapter.

CHAPTER SEVEN

FORCE #4:
MEASURE AND EXPERIMENT

ANALYTICS ARE A major key to your success. Does that word scare you? It shouldn't. Analytics are why I love the digital world—everything you do is measurable! Using analytics gives you a license to fail! Why? Because you can try a different tack, measure the results, analyze what did and didn't work, quickly course-correct, then try again. It's a virtuous cycle.

Once you have identified and converted your whales and built a product pyramid, you should maximize what you've built by tracking key metrics. By keeping an eye on the numbers that matter and running experiments, you can learn what has the most positive impact on your business.

Three legs support your ability to maximize the impact of your pyramid: The first of these is the **dashboard**, which is backward-looking, giving you insights into what has happened in your business.

You can get forward-looking ideas from the other two legs: **running experiments** and **reviewing your customer feedback**.

Leg #1: Building Your Dashboard

One of the first things I do with each new client is create a customized dashboard. The dashboard should contain five to nine key numbers that you track carefully to make sure your strategy is heading in the right direction.

Dashboards are critical. Their purpose is to foster understanding of the numbers driving your business, and to provide a disciplined focus on those numbers. They give you the power to ride winners, tweak or cut losers, and ultimately drive more business. One of my clients saw their profit margins increase by ten points after we implemented a dashboard.

Your dashboard is an organizational leadership tool; you want your whole team to rally around these numbers. If something is off, either good or bad, that's when you do a deep dive to figure out how to further capitalize on the success or reverse the failure. If you see a spike, ask what else you can learn from that number. If something is off, ask yourself, "What is going on? What can we do to course-correct? Or should we take a step back and reset our goals?"

Most people are familiar with executive dashboard best practices: Link them to your strategy, have them cascade down the organization, and have a mix of forward-looking variables (like leads in the sales pipeline) and backward-looking ones (like booked revenue). This all sounds good, but the real learning comes from trying a few things, even if it means making some mistakes. To save you time, here are three good lessons I've picked up over the years on successfully implementing and using dashboards.

1. Focus on About Seven Metrics

Robert Simons, Harvard Business School professor and author of *Seven Strategy Questions,* told me that in his executive education course on performance metrics, he asks all leaders to bring copies of their existing dashboards to class. He awards a prize to the person who has the most metrics—but it's a consolation prize, because this executive is actually the loser.

Simons advocates having only five to nine metrics on your dashboard. There is a temptation to make sure every possible metric appears there, but when a screen is cluttered with too much information, none of it gets the right level of scrutiny, and it's tough to get a feel for the numbers.

I've certainly learned this the hard way. One company I worked with had a twelve-page dashboard (they definitely would have won Professor Simons' prize). You can imagine how difficult it was to detect real issues and separate signal from noise.

To narrow the metrics for your business, take another tip from Simons: Focus on failure. What five to nine things could sink your business if they went wrong?

2. It's a Smoke Detector, Not a Problem Solver
One reason they ended up with twelve pages of metrics is they were trying too hard to make the dashboard more than a dashboard. Remember, the purpose of the dashboard should be to encourage a disciplined review and foster an understanding of the numbers that matter most to your business. When you try to add all possible root causes to your dashboard, it gets unwieldy. The dashboard should function as a smoke detector: It alerts you when something is starting to smolder. When something in the numbers sets off the alarm, then you know it's time to do more analysis to find the root cause and develop a solution.

For example, one client noticed that their traffic had tumbled dramatically, so we did a deep-dive analysis: We looked at sources of traffic (from search, e-mail, social media, etc.), time of day, and devices used (desktop, mobile, tablet). It immediately became clear what the problem was: Traffic was way down on mobile. Clearly the user experience was not optimized for phones, so no one was engaging with that product. We launched an initiative to improve the mobile interface and were thereby able to restore mobile traffic, and thus overall traffic. The dashboard's simplicity helped us catch the problem and start the review.

3. *Minimize Manual Work*

After several years, I realized that I was overemphasizing choosing the "ideal" metrics that perfectly matched our strategy and flowed nicely across the organization, and I wasn't spending enough energy on implementation. As a result, we put a lot more effort into creating the dashboard than using it.

Things got really complicated for my team once when we built a dashboard to support a new segmentation strategy. I wanted to look at performance by custom segment. This meant manual manipulation of the data. As a result, it took the equivalent of two full-time employees just to create the dashboard each week.

Rather than spending tons of time manually piecing together multiple sources of information to calculate the numbers via custom-defined sources, turn to predefined sources like Google Analytics to save you time (more on this soon), and conduct deep analyses when you notice an issue in one of the channels.

A Practical Way to Narrow Down Dashboard Metrics

Identifying the right numbers, creating your dashboard,

and using it to track the most important economic levers to your business can all be accomplished with a practical, seven-step process:

1. **Define your business model.** It's important to understand what business you're in so you know which metrics to track. The excellent article "Business Model Analysis for the Entrepreneur" describes a process for building a "fishbone" diagram of your business model. [30] The diagram methodically breaks down all the drivers of your business. On the following page is a typical fishbone for a traditional magazine publisher:

   As you can see, this diagram breaks down the total revenue of the business into categories, products, and sales methods to show how the publisher makes money.

2. **Determine points of greatest leverage and greatest risk/ uncertainty.** Look at your fishbone and decide where you can leverage small improvements to yield a significant increase in total revenue. Then, look for

---

[30] Richard G. Hamermesh, Paul W. Marshall, and Taz Pirmohamed, "Note on Business Model Analysis for the Entrepreneur," *Harvard Business Review, (Jan. 22, 2002)*, https://hbr.org/product/note-on-business-model-analysis-for-the-entrepreneur/802048-PDF-ENG.

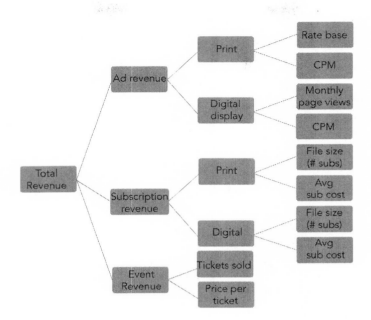

areas of concern: Where is there a large chance of failure? What keeps you up at night? This step provides you with a list of the most important metrics to track on your dashboard. Let's call these items "Key Performance Indicators" (KPIs).

3. **Set goals for each KPI.** For each KPI, decide on a desired outcome. You can base the target on growth over historical performance, benchmarks from similar companies, or another goal.

4. **Set up your dashboard to measure the KPIs.** Figure out how to measure each of the KPIs. If something you want

to track is not measurable, consider finding a proxy. For example, if you want to measure the "number of people who buy something at each live event," but for some reason it's not tracked, use something like "number of items sold per live event." Get creative.

5. **Start tracking and review regularly.** Depending on how rapidly your business moves, check your dashboard daily, weekly, or at least monthly. Get familiar with your numbers. After a few weeks, you should know the key metrics off the top of your head.

6. **Get curious about variances.** Explore both the areas where you exceeded expectations and where you missed the goal. It's helpful to have an analyst who can slice and dice the data for you.

7. **Make changes based on your analysis in step 6.** Then go back to step 5 and repeat the tracking/review process.

Because all businesses evolve, you should go back to step 1 two to three times per year and make sure you are still measuring the right things and have the right targets.

Which Metrics Do I Use?

I encourage you to undertake the exercise above, but if you're looking to get started right away, I have

found the following are the best numbers to track for a
digital membership business:

- Number of active members
- Traffic (unique monthly visitors)
- E-mail capture rate (e-mails captured per
  new, unique visitor)
- Number of new members (or conversion
  rate) by source. (Hint: use the Google
  Analytics sources—direct, organic search,
  social, referral, e-mail, paid search.)
- Free trial pay-up rate (percentage of trial
  users converting to paid members)
- Renewal rate
- Average price

Look at each of these dimensions three ways:

1. Current period (month, week, or day,
   depending on your business).
2. Compared with the same period last year
   if you are an established company, or the
   prior month if you are in high-growth
   mode.
3. Compared with your target (yes, you must
   have a target for each of these).

You can probably think of dozens of metrics that
are missing—and maybe there should be a few substi-
tutions for your business. But look for your five to nine
KPIs—you want to move the needle on those.

The other thing that's really important is tracking. Every page should have a singular goal. If your goal for one particular page is "capture an e-mail," Google Analytics will be able to tell you what percentage of visitors actually gave you their e-mail. If your goal is to capture 4 to 5 percent of traffic and you are at 2 percent, then you need to tweak your approach to improve that. If you overshoot your goal and hit 10 percent, then you would want to ask, "What's working here that I can apply to other parts of my website?"

Avoid the temptation to have more than one goal per website page. Some sites have fifty calls to action (read these twenty articles, watch these auto-play videos, fill in this pop-up form, buy our book, etc.). It's overwhelming. Trust me—one goal at a time.

Take Advantage of Google Analytics to Build Your Dashboard

I've mentioned Google Analytics a few times, so let me expand a bit. The goal of this book is not to make you an expert in Google Analytics, but rather to open your eyes to some practical applications that are sometimes overlooked.

Why Google Analytics? Lots of tools out there can produce complicated displays of website performance data and churn out fancy analytics reports, which may or may not be easy to manipulate. These tools can be expensive and sometimes unhelpful. Google Analytics, on the other hand, can give you the metrics you need, requires only basic technical acumen to use, and is free.

What can Google Analytics do for you? It can easily display many of your key metrics, such as traffic, conversions, and e-mail capture. Google Analytics' many features can be overwhelming for beginners, so a good way to ease into using it is to look at a few of the standard reports, which cover your traffic and its sources. The other thing that you'll want to set up is cold tracking, which allows you to see who is buying things or providing their e-mail address.

You can use Google Analytics to understand where your traffic comes from and what causes visitors to take actions on your website, such as giving you an e-mail address or signing up for a product.

My advice: **don't waste your time setting up Google Analytics yourself.** While it's pretty straightforward, it is a time drain. Hire a freelancer who can get it done for you in a day. Just make sure you tell him or her what you want to track, which we will cover shortly.

With any analytics freelancer, you need to be clear about the business function you hope to achieve. If you just hire someone and say, "Hey, set up Google Analytics for us," you will end up with very basic, general reports—probably not what you're looking for.

But if you specify a limited number of key metrics that reflect the drivers of your business (which you should be able to do once you set up your dashboard), you'll obtain information that can make a real difference for you. What's more, once you've clearly identified what needs to be measured, hiring a freelancer should be a much more streamlined and inexpensive process.

There are two keys to successful implementation of Google Analytics (or any software). First, you need **business acumen**, meaning that someone knowledgeable needs to identify the metrics that matter most to the business—someone who can get inside the CEO or owner's head and know, "These are the crucial numbers and I'm going to be looking at them all the time." This person will be less interested in the technology and more in the "So what?"

Second, you need someone who will do the **actual implementation**. A lot of off-the-shelf software like Google Analytics is very simple to use, and you could have an entry-level person or freelancer with basic technical skills set it up.

You should focus on the business, and leave the technical side to the technical experts.

Leg #2: Running Experiments (A/B Split Tests)

When a number on your dashboard is off track, or you have a brainstorm for a creative new idea, then it's time to turn to the second leg of optimization: A/B split tests. A/B split tests involve creating two versions of a page or form and dividing traffic between the two so you can measure which one performs better. You can test all types of things, from irresistible offers to sign-up methods, checkout methods, landing pages, and more.

How do A/B split tests work? Let's say that e-mail sign-ups are one of our key metrics and that they are trailing our target. We'll do a deep dive, asking open-ended questions to discover how we can improve, such as, "What's the best way to capture more e-mail leads on our page? Is it better to collect e-mails from pop-up forms or embedded forms? Is it better to give away a coupon or a free white paper? Is it better to ask for just the e-mail address and then go back later for additional information about the subscriber, or to request three or four additional pieces of information during the sign-up process?"

The key is to ask a bunch of questions and realize that there's never a right or wrong answer. Smart people could argue either side of the debate. The only way to practically settle the dispute is to run the A/B test.

Next, you would create two different versions of your e-mail capture form; send half the traffic to one and half the traffic to the other, and observe which one performs better. Which attracts more e-mail sign-ups as a percentage of total traffic?

Many tools can help you with this. Google Experiments is a free option, and there are tons of other off-the-shelf software applications as well. This is something that can be set up in a day or two by someone who knows what he or she is doing—provided, again, that you tell them the key metrics to measure.

Building Consistent Testing Processes Can Be Fun
When people hear the terms *process mapping* or *operational improvements*, they often think, *Boring!* But having consistent processes is important no matter what business you're in: You need repeatable processes for efficiency and scalability. Even so, it doesn't need to be boring! There are two ways to make building consistent processes fun.

First, make defining the process enjoyable. An example of this can be seen in the movie *The Founder*, starring Michael Keaton, which chronicles the real-life story of Ray Kroc and the building of the McDonald's empire.

For those unfamiliar with the story, here is a quick overview: Ray Kroc is a serial entrepreneur who is mesmerized by the "speedy service system" developed by the McDonald brothers in San Bernardino, California. Ray convinces the brothers to let him franchise McDonald's. The brand takes off.

In one scene, there is a great visual example of A/B split testing. The McDonald brothers turn a tennis court into a prototype for a restaurant (by sketching in cooking equipment and walls with chalk). The goal: Make their kitchen as efficient as possible so they can provide "fast food."

They run drills with a stopwatch and clipboard to see which setup and workflow lead to the most efficient process. Before building the kitchen, they tested numerous options to find the right one—and had fun doing it.

Your team will get excited about testing once they feel that process design can be creative—that it's like a game. You can gamify your A/B split tests to make the process enjoyable. I usually offer prizes to client teams who win the test.

The second way to get your team excited about it is to remind them that if you have a more efficient process for the routine stuff, it leaves more time for them to focus on more creative, strategic activities.

Leg #3: Customer Feedback

The final leg to focus on is your members' reaction to you. Here's the secret: Don't be defensive. Just *listen*! I know from personal experience how emotionally invested you are in a new product launch. To hear negative customer feedback can be gut-wrenching after all that hard work.

However, you should thrive on this feedback. It's actually a gift. It's like you're getting the answers to the test beforehand. For one client, right after launch we had a 70 percent free trial pay-up rate (which is really good), but we were able to boost it up to 77 percent within a month because we implemented some straightforward fixes based on initial customer feedback. Imagine getting a "free" 10 percent increase (i.e., an increase of 7 percentage points over the base of 70 percent) in your revenues in just thirty days! That's the power of feedback.

The best way to measure customer feedback is through a Net Promoter Score (NPS). Essentially this means asking, "Would you recommend us to a friend?" Chances are you have responded to a survey that asked you how likely you were to recommend a product or service to someone you know. The company was probably conducting an NPS survey.

NPS is one number with a lot of power. It is a great way to measure the loyalty of your customers. Fred Reichheld of Bain and Company developed this methodology, and Bain's research shows a direct correlation between NPS and revenue. Companies with the highest scores in their category **grow at over twice the rate** of the category average.

The beauty of NPS is that it is easy, practical, and actionable. You simply ask customers, "How likely is it that you would recommend [your product/brand] to a friend or colleague?" Then provide a scale from 10 ("Extremely likely") to 1 ("Not likely at all").

Anyone who responds 9 or 10 is considered a "**Promoter**." This group, according to the research, has the highest retention rate, profitability, and cost efficiency (they're not tying up your resources complaining!). They also serve as brand advocates and generate word-of-mouth referrals for you.

Anyone who responds 8 or 7 is "**Passive**."

Anyone who responds 6 or lower is a "**Detractor**." (Yes, we live in a world of grade inflation, so a 6 is bad). This group tends to have low retention rates and is costly to serve. They may also damage your reputation in the marketplace with negative word of mouth.

Your Net Promoter Score is equal to the percentage of people who are Promoters (9 or above) minus the percentage of people who are Detractors (6 or below).

What Is a "Good" Score?

That's a bit of a trick question. Best-in-class firms such as Apple, Amazon, and Costco have high scores around 80, while average businesses have a score of 10–20. However, what's most important is to benchmark your current score and create a game plan for improving your score—and thus your growth potential.

What to Measure on Paid Digital Membership Sites

For paid digital memberships, I have found it useful to measure NPS at various stages along the customer funnel. This will provide insights into how to move customers along in their journey.

For one client, we divided the universe into four groups:

1. People who gave us their e-mail but did not sign up for a trial
2. People who signed up for a trial but did not pay for a membership
3. First-year members
4. Year 2+ members

You might assume that NPS gradually increased from Groups 1 to 4. However, we were surprised to find out that the group with the lowest NPS was actually Group 3. Upon analyzing the free response answers and speaking with a few customers in this bracket, we learned that we had to do a better job with content discovery. Customers were excited during the trial period and spent time exploring the content. After a few weeks, however, these customers were a bit lost and needed some nudging to engage with the content.

The NPS score showed us what we needed to focus on and steered us toward a solution. Once you have zeroed in on a problem and implemented a remedy, reexamine your NPS to see if it had the effect you expected. Once we designed a better search tool for this client, their NPS improved.

How to Implement Net Promoter Score

There are some practical ways to implement NPS in your business to drive growth in paid digital memberships and other digital revenue streams.

If your platform doesn't automatically monitor NPS, here is a quick and dirty idea: Use something like Google Forms or Survey Monkey to create the NPS survey (as described above). Create one survey for each of your segments (trial customers, first-year customers, long-time customers, etc.), and send it out to a sample of customers within each segment. While segmentation is critical, be careful about segmenting too finely. You'll need at least thirty responses per segment to get meaningful data.

Gathering More Actionable Data from NPS

Along with the "would you recommend us" question, you should ask an open-ended question such as "What is the primary reason for the score you just gave us?" or "What is the most important improvement that would make you rate us closer to a 10?" The answers to these questions can provide you with specific action items you can implement to increase loyalty.

You may also want to ask for permission to follow up with respondents and collect their contact information. If you go this route, take special care to reach out to all the Detractors—they'll be expecting your call.

Open-ended answers can help you develop new products. When the people giving you high scores (your whales) tell you how you could do even better, those suggestions should guide your next moves. Can you address their needs with a new feature on an existing product? A new product altogether? A change in the way you communicate with your customers? This principle of focusing on your whales—the people who are giving you nines and tens, who are saying good things about you and probably sending you leads without you knowing it—will drive growth. If you listen to their comments and provide them with what they ask for, your business will reap the benefits.

Make sure you communicate your results broadly across departments in your business. Create a sense of urgency. Take action on what your customers are telling you. For one company, Bain found that over a customer's lifetime, a Promoter generated $9,500 more in profits than a Detractor! There is a real upside to getting started ASAP.

How Do You Define Success?

It's important to use these tools to set goals, and to define what success means for your company. To do so, get every key member of your team into a room at least once every quarter to review the dashboard and set goals for success. Study the dashboard, the test results, and your NPS scores. Go through them number by number and ask your key team members, "Which of these numbers can we improve? Which initiatives can we improve? Here are our key metrics; what kinds of experiments do we need to run?" This is also the time to review experiments that are not working, and correct your course.

Go through everything and discuss where there's room to do better. We know we can't focus on all seven things at the same time, but **where do we think the most opportunity is?** Where can we launch new initiatives that will lead to better results? Where will we get the biggest bang for our buck?

This process will get your team engaged, which you need to do to discover opportunities.

When to Pull the Plug on an Experiment

How do you know when it's time to jettison offerings that don't work, and what lessons can you learn from the experience?

You want to create a culture in your business in which it's okay to launch new products, even though they may not all be smash hits—but you don't want to bleed so much that you run out of cash. You want to give your team a license to fail, yet you want to avoid pulling the plug too quickly without seeing experiments through. Maybe the first e-mail didn't go well. Did you give it enough time? Did you get people used to seeing this new product?

But you don't want to sink time and energy into failing products, either. So, when *is* it time to pull the plug? How do you set boundaries?

One way is to establish a budget. Set aside a pool of money that you are willing put at risk. You say, "We are going to give this idea $50,000. If we run out of money and still haven't hit any of our goals, it's time to walk away."

Another way is to follow your NPS. This is a great indicator because it comes directly from your customers.

A declining NPS indicates negative word of mouth and little sharing, so you need to act.

If you have launched a new product and after a couple of rounds of surveys your customers are responding with negative feedback, then you know it's time to rethink the product. Read the comments from the detractors and the promoters, which will give you an indication of what's working and not working. If after a few adjustments the NPS isn't trending upward, it's time to pull the plug.

A third way to set boundaries is to acknowledge the opportunity cost of time. If another idea comes along that has greater upside with less risk, and your results with a current product experiment are mediocre, then it's time to correct your course.

Innovation starts with measurement of key numbers and running experiments. This can be a fun process for you and your team. Ultimately, this approach will optimize your business model and spur growth.

Next up: How to bring it all together with the right level of support.

CHAPTER EIGHT

FORCE #5:
CREATE BANDWIDTH

THIS CHAPTER IS all about building out the structures you need to implement the previous four forces. My team recently analyzed hundreds of niche media companies and calculated how much money publishers are leaving on the table in terms of digital opportunity. The figure we arrived at exceeds the jackpot of any lottery in history: businesses are leaving *over $2 billion per year* on the table.

I've asked many clients why this is happening. Almost unanimously, they answer with some variation of, "We just don't have the time/money/know-how to successfully launch a better digital platform."

I started my company to help niche publishers overcome that particular objection. I've been in media for a while now, and I get it. I know a lot of publishers are stretched really thin, but I also know from firsthand experience that you can *find* the bandwidth. I'll show you three options for doing so in this chapter.

1. Pruning
2. Hiring New Employees
3. Using Partners

Option #1: Pruning

The goal of pruning is to free up capacity by eliminating tasks and processes that do not contribute meaningfully to the success of your business. In my experience, it's possible for most businesses to eliminate as much as 20 percent of what they do in order to free up their resources so that they have the capacity to work on new ideas. Look at your workload and ask yourself, "Have we maximized the use of our time and assets?"

It can be daunting, but it will pay off. I realized the value of pruning the first time I had to fire someone I'd inherited when I joined a company. I knew this employee had to go because he was having a negative effect on the team, and my job as a manager was to keep a high-quality team.

Still, I was nervous. One thought was keeping me up at night: How am I going to cover the workload if I'm down a full-time employee? I soon realized, however, that half of the forty hours per week this employee was working could have been thrown in the trash. He was spending twenty hours each week doing things a certain way because that was the way we'd always done them—but there was really no business benefit to continuing to do those things at all. So not only was he not performing, but after firing him I came to realize that much of what he was doing was largely unnecessary. This prompted me to ask: What are my team and I spending time on that is not contributing to our growth? Is there time we can free up by eliminating some unnecessary work?

Perform audits to figure out if you're spending time on things that aren't benefiting your business. You should regularly look at your team members' individual outputs to see how they're spending their time and whether their activities are contributing to your bottom line. This means sitting down and asking them, "What are you doing every day?"

The Five Ds of Time Management

Another important aspect of pruning is improving your time management. There's a process you and your team can use to help you prioritize things, freeing up time and money to devote to growing your digital revenue.

1. Do It
2. Delegate It
3. Diminish It
4. Delay It
5. Delete It

For the most important and urgent items on your list, don't procrastinate—**Do it**. Just get these activities done. For things that are lower on the priority list, you have a choice among the remaining four Ds. You can

Delegate the task to someone else. Another option is to **Diminish it**, meaning reduce the scope of the project. You can also **Delay it**—push the deadline out on something that is not important enough to spend your time on right now. Finally, you can **Delete it**—decide *not* to do it at all.

If you find it challenging to go through this exercise yourself—if it's difficult for you to look objectively at how worthwhile your projects are—then talk with a board member or hire an executive coach.

You are going to have to coach your team on this, because everyone thinks that everything they're doing is mission-critical. But there are *always* activities that aren't producing returns. More important, there is likely high-value work your team doesn't have time for because they're focusing on unproductive activities.

When you can see that some of your activities are causing you to miss opportunities, you know it's time to prune. How can you do this for yourself? More critically, how can you get your team to prune their own projects?

One of the gravest mistakes many organizations make is to assume that change will flow naturally throughout the organization. But it's not so. Change is hard. There is an entire field called "change management" that is devoted to motivating teams to think differently so they can grow.

First, get your leaders on board at every level. Pruning starts with the C-suite and should cascade downward. It's not enough for your CEO and CMO to want to go digital; the head of your sales team needs to be excited as well. Otherwise, he or she won't find the time to support digital efforts.

The importance of communication cannot be overstated. Transparency is key to success. Communicate with your team early and often about every step of your digital transformation. Be patient with your team and help them when they need it; change takes time. Your new plan for the business, whether it's going digital or something else entirely, requires your team to break down everything they know and reconstruct it in an entirely new way.

Be clear, be open, and be prepared. By pruning unnecessary work from your agenda, you can open bandwidth and focus on opportunities for growth.

Option #2: Hiring New Employees

Hiring full-time employees can create bandwidth, and this is a long-term solution. But I caution you against rushing to hire people. I recommend bringing people in-house *only after you've gotten set up and have a proven business model.* Why?

Hiring people is expensive. Here are some common annual salaries for the people you'll need to bring in to launch a digital membership program:

- Product Manager $100,000
- Digital Marketing Manager $95,000
- Developer $77,000
- Web Designer $73,000
- Digital Editor $62,000

Add all that up and you're looking at $407,000! On top of that, there are a lot of hidden costs to hiring an employee.

- Hiring and training
- Taxes and insurance
- Benefits
- Paid vacation
- Workstation and equipment, etc.

These extra expenses easily double the required investment in each employee. Hiring staff takes a lot of work and time commitment, and at the end of all of that, new hires can have a short shelf life: the average tenure for a millennial employee is just over one year. So before hiring anyone full-time, make sure you have a proven business model that can support the expense.

Don't get me wrong, the long-term answer *is* employees, and there are lots of benefits you get from them, such as camaraderie, long-term relationships, and long-term thinking. You get more loyalty and commitment from full-time employees. But first, you need to prove the business model before incurring those high costs.

So, once you're up and running, how do you know it is time to bring the work in-house? Here's a checklist:

- **Business model proven.** The revenue stream has caught on.
- **Processes worked out and documented.** You've codified how you

do business. You use this documentation to train new hires and get them off to a solid start.

- **Multiple products can fill capacity of full-time employee.** You've built out your product pyramid and have enough work to keep your new employee busy and engaged.

Once you've checked off all those boxes, it's time to start hiring. For publishers operating on a tight budget and trying out ideas, however, it's better to hire external partners for specific projects rather than bringing people onto your staff full-time.

Option #3: Using Partners

Do you find that you have growth ideas, but your ability to implement them is limited by budget and time? Why not find a trusted partner who can help you step away from the day-to-day and launch new initiatives? You can bring successful initiatives in-house once they are proven, and avoid expensive investments in experiments that may or may not work out.

Using external help for specific projects allows you to innovate and experiment on a low budget with limited risk. It also allows you to tap into experts who would be too expensive to hire on a full-time basis.

You have to be careful and do your due diligence before selecting partners. There can be flakiness, overpromising, and under-delivering. I've created some best practices to help guide you in selecting valuable partners:

Look for Thought Leaders. This is the best way to separate the wannabes from the real deal. If a company's leadership team regularly speaks at key industry events, publishes original content, and has a strong point of view on the subject at hand, it's more likely that they'll deliver results for you as they have done for other clients in the past.

If someone is not a thought leader, they're more likely to be a hack. On one occasion early in my career I realized (too late) that I had hired a freelance developer who fit that description. He seemed knowledgeable at first, but I later realized he was more like a teacher who didn't really know the material and was just staying one day ahead of the classroom. He rarely understood the business requirements of projects I tasked him with, and he often resorted to Googling our questions to get an answer. Once we realized we were paying him to get educated, we ended the contract and moved on to a real thought leader.

Word of Mouth. One of the best ways to get connected with a talented partner is to ask your network whom they have been happy to work with in the past. Talk to your colleagues at other companies, ask for recommendations on social media, inquire with leaders of trade groups or associations, or browse through shared connections on LinkedIn. With word-of-mouth recommendations, you almost always know ahead of time what kind of relationship you're walking into.

Focus on Business Acumen. If a partner lacks business acumen, you're going to be stuck holding their hand through every project. There are a lot of great developers and designers out there, but many of them are just order takers. They're going to give you exactly what they think you want, so if you're not always *exactly* clear on what you want, you may lose time and money going in the wrong direction.

Someone with business acumen, on the other hand, can grasp the reason behind the specifications and make educated guesses. A partner like that is going to be much more self-sufficient.

Find out: Can they tell you how their projects fit into your overall company goals? Does their track record include statistics that show how their contributions directly improved other companies' bottom lines? If you're hiring help for audience development, for example, and a prospective agency tells you that they used paid retargeting ads to boost digital subscriptions by 200 percent without increasing overall marketing spend, that's a big deal.

You need partners who can anticipate the next big trend in your industry. Probe to see how forward-thinking each candidate is by asking them what industry trends they think are most important to watch over the next year. You need to hire partners who are looking ahead to ensure that you do not lag behind digital trends.

Intellectual Curiosity. One other critical "soft skill" you need to assess during the partner screening process is intellectual curiosity. According to *Harvard Business Review*, there are three main factors that affect a person's ability to manage complex situations: their IQ, their EQ (emotional intelligence quotient), and CQ— their level of curiosity.[31] Their strengths in these soft skills make it possible for them to function as problem solvers, original thinkers, and strong managers, and to keep pace with the ever-evolving digital space.

Ask them about their aspirations, what they do or don't like doing professionally, or what industry conferences they've attended recently. Ask them what they are currently reading, or which podcasts they subscribe to. Look up their LinkedIn profiles and scan for accomplishments that demonstrate a passion for learning, such as education, advancement, interests, etc.

Structure Deals to Minimize Losses. Make sure you structure your deals with partners that minimize the risk for you. Most people think there are just two models: pay by the hour or pay by the project. I've found a more balanced model that is superior to either of the standard options: a retainer with an easy opt-out. You pay a small retainer up front, with most of the payoff dependent on performance. Everyone's incentives are aligned, there's no motivation to cut corners, and there's budget certainty. You agree to pay a set amount per month, and you agree on the scope of projects and on milestones. While the rate is based on an estimated number of hours each month, no

---

[31] Tomas Chamorro-Premuzic, "Curiosity Is as Important as Intelligence," *Harvard Business Review*, August 27, 2014, https://hbr.org/2014/08/curiosity-is-as-important-as-intelligence.

timesheets are kept. *The important thing is to focus on meeting milestones.* You have the right to fire the partner at the end of the term if milestones are not met or quality is a concern.

We usually offer this type of model to our clients: a modest monthly retainer, with a bonus structure based on a percentage of revenue created. This way we're in it together. We keep the risk low for the client, and we can both enjoy the upside of success. For one client, we delivered a product whose revenues were literally twelve times higher than our forecast.

•••

If you follow the processes in this chapter, you can free up the necessary bandwidth to execute the five forces needed to monetize your content online. With a strong strategy built on these five forces, you can effectively tell employees and partners alike what you want and vet them based on their ability to give it to you.

Of course one of the most valuable tools for creating extra bandwidth—both for yourself and for your organization—is technology. It's important to remember, however, that the technological tools you employ are less important than the business objectives those tools are meant to accomplish. Before you run out and embrace the newest tech fad, you need to think strategically about *how* you're going to use it, and *what* you're going to use it to achieve.

CHAPTER NINE

STRATEGY AND TECHNOLOGY

IF YOU TAKE nothing else away from this chapter, remember this: *Don't spend a dime on technology until you have a plan.*

Ideally your implementation of the five forces should be in motion even before you begin asking people to buy your content. You can set up a paywall, but if your content isn't positioned correctly to optimize both your value proposition to the reader and the return on investment for you, you would be better off waiting.

Technology without a strategy doesn't get you anywhere, and because it's costly and time-consuming, it can even be detrimental to your business. The most common mistake publishers make is spending money on technology before forming a strategy. That is a disaster waiting to happen. First you need to commit to the five forces of a successful digital membership strategy that I've outlined in this book; only then should you start making technology purchases that fit into your strategy.

I learned this lesson the hard way. Early in my career, I started a new job and inherited a to-do list. One of the items on the agenda was implementing a new content management system (CMS). The company was already three-quarters of the way through the process. Eager to check items off the to-do list, I thought, "Let's roll up our sleeves and get it done."

I helped finalize the deal for the new CMS, on which we spent $100,000, plus six months of implementation, which distracted the team. In the end, however, it had almost no impact whatsoever on the business, because the new CMS didn't do anything meaningfully better.

If I could do it over, I would pause that project and ask, "What's our reason for getting a new CMS? Is it part of a bigger strategy?" Instead, I let the train continue down the wrong track. We lost money and time, and the next time I needed money for a project, I faced a lot of skepticism.

I learned a valuable lesson from this experience: **If you're going to spend money on technology, it has to be coupled with a strategy for *getting new customers* or *keeping existing customers*.**

If you're an owner and you invest your hard-earned cash in a significant technological upgrade, the stakes are high. And if you're in a difficult situation, and you're spending money to get out of the hole and get on a growth trajectory, the stakes are even higher. You get only so many at-bats, and you don't get too many chances to make big mistakes. And if you're an executive, rather than an owner, choosing a technology investment that flops could be a fireable offense. It's certainly tempting to think the latest software is all you need, but technology doesn't work in a vacuum. Technology is just a tool; it doesn't solve innovation problems by itself. Unless you have a plan to make that software work for the *needs of your business*, you're going to waste time and money, and you'll hamper your business.

It's also dangerous to hire a consultant without a strategy. Following any consultant's blueprint blindly can get you into trouble.

If an agency does not consider how *their* blueprint and their technology are relevant to *your* business, you may wind up spending a bunch of money and distracting your team from day-to-day work—and in the end, the technology may not even work for you because your brand is different from what the consultant is used to, or your whales are different, or their technology is five years out of date.

In one case I witnessed, an established magazine signed with a vendor that claimed their technology platform and approach could generate a lot of money online. The publication spent $150,000 to move all their content over to this platform ... and it didn't work. The problem was that the vendor didn't think the business model through; they treated all content equally. They just moved all of the magazine's content over to their standard platform (the same one they use for *all* clients) without considering the magazine's unique value proposition to its whales. For example, the way pet lovers want to consume content is likely different from how accountants would like to, and this was not considered at all by the vendor, who tried to shoehorn the client into a "one size fits all" solution.

Sadly, that magazine's core business model fell apart in the course of the transition because they were so busy working on an expensive new system that they didn't properly cater to their best customers: Their readers didn't like the new interface and were confused about why the changes had been made. Far from achieving their goal of converting loyal customers into paying customers, the magazine *lost* their existing traffic.

The lesson to be learned here is that launching new technology without a plan can be disruptive to your customers, which can ultimately destroy your whales' brand loyalty.

•••

There are also many common and costly marketing mistakes that can be made when strategy is not clearly defined. For example, an executive I know who had never paid for advertising was approached by the company's board, which asked, "Why don't you do any Facebook advertising?" So he jumped at it. They hired an agency and spent $125,000 before they realized that *their whales weren't on Facebook*. So their ads only led to nonqualified customers signing up for free trials and then cancelling. That company didn't take the time to set up a strategy, and instead they jumped on a quick-fix marketing tactic that backfired. That CEO ended up getting fired because of his inability to understand digital. Technology and marketing tactics without a strategy behind them are not solutions. Neither is a consultant with a one-size-fits-all approach. It's vital to come up with a strategy and a product that are specific to your market, and to make sure that you have the right business model in place before launching any new technology.

•••

Using the five forces I've outlined, I'm confident you can come up with a strategy that will lead you to the right marketing and technology plan in a strategic, customer-oriented way. I don't want you to shoehorn products or marketing channels into your plan. I hope I've helped you to create a strategy that informs those choices. Maybe Facebook ads *are* great for your business, and maybe they're not. Double-check that you have a true strategy and not just a list of tactics and financial goals.

Some people think, "I have a marketing strategy. I can target my customers on Google and Facebook. I know my customers are between the ages of twenty-five and forty-five and predominantly female. People in that demographic group are on Facebook, so I can find them there."

That's not a strategy—it's a tactic. There's probably a reason that you consider that particular audience on Facebook valuable, and we'd want to explore that. But relying on a tactic as your strategy is risky. Facebook could change its algorithms. The supply and demand could change, causing the cost of those Facebook ads to go way up, which would affect your ROI. A better platform could come along. On the other side of the coin, there could be many similar customers who *aren't* on Facebook, and by focusing too intently on social media, you could miss them.

If you've discovered that a particular tactic works for you today, that's a good first step. But you need to think more strategically about that insight.

If you've ever heard or caught yourself using any of the following, or variations of them, to describe your strategy, it's a good indicator that what you are doing is *not* **a strategy—it's a goal, a tactic, or a to-do list item**.

"Our strategy is to use a target list of ad words." Nope, that's a tactic.

"Our strategy is to hit our budget." Nope, that's a goal.

"Our strategy is to implement the best CMS platform to provide content to our visitors." Nope, that's a to-do list item.

"Our strategy is segmentation on Facebook, on which we get a handsome ROI." Nope. Tactic.

•••

I started my company to help content creators succeed in the digital world. Armed with these five forces I've shown you, you're well on your way to a thriving digital presence. If you feel you'd like to continue the conversation with me and my company in order to learn more and receive guidance on implementing these tools, read on and I'll let you know who my company serves, and how I can help you implement these lessons.

CHAPTER TEN

SHOULD WE CONTINUE
THE CONVERSATION?

BY NOW YOU understand why it's important to adapt to the digital world and make money directly from your whales without relying on advertising to sustain you. You've learned the five forces of a successful digital strategy. You know that it is important to have a plan before spending money on a solution. If you feel you'd like me to guide you through this process, let's explore whether we're a good fit.

Many content creators struggle to balance their need to operate their business day to day with the imperative to try new things to grow their business. My company's services enable you to launch new digital initiatives without distracting you from your daily operations. When the new programs start to make money, we integrate them into your system and your employees' hands so that we can work on the next experiment to keep your business growing.

We can help you:

- Grow your digital income 50 percent or more
- Sustain growth with our robust and easy-to-implement innovation and marketing methodology
- Eliminate time spent researching and stressing over changes in digital media
- Avoid making a poor technology investment that could cause problems

I have two main goals for my clients: I want you to make a lot of money, but just as important, I want you to **feel empowered to direct the strategy** of your business so that you can foster its growth and be proud of the amazing content you and your team produce.

Who We Serve

My whales are publishers and media production companies. I work directly with CEOs, owners, partners, principals, senior executives, and general managers at these companies. I also serve professional services firms, business consulting firms, and data aggregators. Any business that has content, be it written, video, or audio, that its whales consider valuable can monetize that content to great success.

We might be a good match if you answer "yes" to the following questions:

Can you envision a bright future for your brand? Content creators who are just trying to squeeze the last cash they can out of a dying business aren't right for us.

On the other hand, if you're looking forward and are excited about the future, we can help. Even if your business is in trouble, if you can envision that five years from now, you can be reinvigorated, then consider reaching out to us for help transforming your company for the future.

Let's imagine it's the early twentieth century and you run a small country. The car has been invented, but in your country, everyone is riding around on horses, and it's a pain in the neck to get from point A to point B. What do you do? Do you make better horse paths and breed faster horses and come up with better training techniques? Or do you say it's time to adopt the car?

The people I can provide the most value to are those who feel it's time to adopt the car.

Do you value patience and persistence? Our five-force process takes perseverance; results take time. This process is going to yield substantial quick wins, but to fully benefit from our system you must embrace a multiyear time horizon.

Do you see failures as learning opportunities? Experimentation and testing are absolutely necessary to our strategy. We know that there are things we don't know, so we conduct A/B tests to show us what we need to fix. If you're a perfectionist you may not like that, but to make more money online you have to be able to tolerate some failures and treat them as learning opportunities.

How committed are you to using new digital channels to drive your growth? In order to make this transition, you need to believe in the power of digital and really want to capitalize on it.

Does your business possess a large repository of valuable information that, if reconfigured, could further benefit your existing market or ancillary markets? The bulk of what we do involves repurposing existing evergreen content into a product pyramid that meets your whales' needs.

Do you wonder what to prioritize to achieve the highest ROI with the least risk and lowest investment? We can help companies that are unsure how to proceed into the online realm, that have questions about what steps to take, and are seeking guidance.

Would you be interested if someone you trusted could tell you how to harness your existing content and the most powerful motivations of your customers, in order to drive growth of 50 percent or more for your business? Our clients experience amazing growth by following our strategies to create a thriving business centered on their whales.

Services We Offer

Following my own advice, I built my product pyramid by focusing on my whales— small to mid-size publishers and content creators who are nervous about their future, whose businesses may be declining, and who need to grow. Here are the products and services my company offers to solve those problems:

Tier 1: Free and Low-Cost Content

My company's blog on sterlingwoodsgroup.com has a ton of content that addresses issues publishers face. The book you are reading right now also fits into this tier, as it provides a primer to the five forces of online growth for publishers.

Tier 2: In-Person Workshop/Keynote Speech

I can come in and speak to a company's management team or employees about our system for driving digital revenue in that company's niche, and I can answer questions during that session. This tier provides a sharing of knowledge and a Q&A opportunity. We tailor the workshop to your specific needs.

Tier 3: Detailed Digital Road Map ("Trail Map")

This solution includes custom development of a specific digital product and marketing plan for your business, grounded in all five forces from this book. As part of our diagnostic, we

- run a kickoff brainstorming session with key employees;
- interview and survey your whales, and develop a new value proposition for you;
- analyze your current products, websites,

marketing practices, and key performance metrics; and
- review the competitive environment.

We then develop a detailed digital road map—a concise list of the initiatives with the greatest likelihood of success. We typically implement revenue growth ideas worth over ten times the amount of our fees! We review this plan via an interactive in-person workshop.

Tier 4: Road Map with Implementation Coaching ("Trail Guide")

We start with the Tier 3 solution and then add ongoing coaching to ensure successful execution. We get together every two weeks to run a workshop.

Our goals for ongoing coaching are threefold: First, we want to transfer our knowledge and experience so your team can grow. Some ways we do this include mocking up wireframes to demonstrate some of the key conversion principles, drafting sample e-mails that meet best practices, suggesting a dashboard and learning agenda, and offering constructive feedback on collateral produced by your team.

Second, we want to be trusted problem solvers. While the coaching workshops are biweekly, any client is welcome to call or e-mail us at any time with any question or problem. We'll help you work through it. In every coaching workshop, we'll review the progress on key initiatives, the dashboard, and the results of A/B split tests.

SHOULD WE CONTINUE THE CONVERSATION? | 149

Third, quite frankly, we want to hold you accountable! How many times have you taken a fancy PowerPoint deck from a consultant, stuck it on a shelf, and let it gather dust? How many times have you come back from a conference all fired up, and then done nothing with any of the concepts, methods, or strategies you learned? It would sadden us to work with you to develop an amazing growth plan, only for nothing to come of it in the end. That's not our style. We want you to ring the register after working with us.

Tier 5: Full Valet Service—Trailblazer Lab

This is the top of our pyramid. If you opt for the full valet service, we handle the entire process with you. We go through all five forces and implement them for you. We start with a diagnostic, in which we help you find your whales and develop a slate of initiatives to grow and protect your business, including sales and marketing optimization projects, product refinement and new product development, and predictive content to determine what will sell.

Then we figure out how we are going to attract and convert your whales, what other products we are going to sell them, and what tests and experiments we need to run to ensure success. Finally, we put together a team to design and build the website for you, and continue to keep an eye on all five forces.

For this tier, my company takes a percentage of the upside so we can keep our fees low to build this for you, and to put skin in the game so our incentives are aligned. While we're getting you up and running we work at our costs—and often below them—and then we make money together as partners, sharing the revenue from our success.

We're unique in that we take really low upfront payment and have a revenue sharing model. We operate in this manner because we're confident in the results we produce. This way clients can get in with limited upfront investment, and we all can share the upside.

Let me walk you through what we did for *Brew Your Own* magazine, one of our Tier 5 clients whom we love working with.

We started by brainstorming value proposition ideas with the senior team: What content would homebrewers be willing to pay for? What problems could we solve for them, and what emotional benefits could we bring to them?

We then interviewed a bunch of their "whales" (serious homebrewers) and followed up with a survey. Their whales were so engaged that we got over a thousand responses.

Based on our analysis of the research, and our review of competitive sites, we came up with a new value proposition, and we completely redesigned the entire online experience to fulfill this promise. Most important, we determined what was going to be free and what would be paid content. For example, all beginner content and resource tools (like calculators and charts) would be free. In-depth content like recipes or Q&A with the brewing expert ("Mr. Wizard") became for members only.

We developed a launch campaign for the new membership, which included e-mail marketing and on-site promotion, and even today we continue to run digital marketing efforts and make product enhancements based on customer feedback (like the NPS survey). We also run A/B split tests all the time to increase member conversion and retention. We help cross-sell members to events and upsell print subscribers into the membership. Basically, we put into play all five forces described in this book.

We only take on a small handful of Trailblazer Lab members each year.

If you are interested, you can learn more about it and apply at:

https://sterlingwoodsgroup.com/lab

What to Expect When You Reach Out to Us

If you want to know more, give me a call. **Here's my number: 617-544-7883.**

That's a direct line to me. If you choose to call us, you will speak to the author of this book. I will not pass you off to a lower-level employee or have you talk to a sales rep—you're going to talk to me. For my business, it's important to build a strong relationship with each client—after all, if we do work together, we will be like partners.

The first call with me lasts around thirty minutes. I will ask you to tell me about your business, and I'll listen so that I can understand your company and your vision. Then I'll ask a few questions about where you think you are now and where you want to be. Based on your answers, if I think we can help you bridge that gap, I'll suggest which of our services would be the most effective way to get you there.

After that call, if we both agree there's a mutual fit, I will send you a proposal reflecting our understanding of your situation, your aspirations, and specifically what we will do over what time period and at what tier.

After we send you a proposal, we'll either meet in person or hop on a video call and I'll go through the proposal with you, making sure it's crystal clear and answering any questions you may have. If you need buy-in from co-owners, we're happy to speak with them, too.

Our fundamental belief at Sterling Woods is that brands should focus on what they're best at—creating content—and we should focus on what *we're* best at, which is strategy, product development, and marketing. We don't produce the content for you, but we can help you come up with a strategy and deploy it for you in a way that's going to make a lot of money.

Innovating can certainly feel risky, but we help our clients come up with a process to minimize risk. We know it's going to work if you just try it, and that there are opportunities for your business to grow.

It has been a pleasure to take you along on this expedition. If you're interested in continuing the journey and discussing these matters further, call me for a thirty-minute talk, and we'll see if we can help you reach your goals. **617-544-7883**

ACKNOWLEDGEMENTS

To my wife and daughter, Kate and Helena Ristagno, for their support and inspiration. To my extended family for their encouragement: My parents, Rob and Diane Ristagno; and my siblings, Andrea and Rob Horst, and Jim and Kristina Ristagno.

To Carolyn Gimbrone, Bob Bowsza, and Bryan Gage for feedback and improvements to the manuscript.

To various mentors, colleagues, and friends who have helped in some way to bring this book to life: Todd Berman, Nancy Brand, Marlissa Briggett, Rebekah Darksmith, Andrew Davis, Kristi Dougherty, Matt Frucci, Lori Galvin, Joel Gluck, Patrick Hereford, Beth Ineson, Monika Katoch, David McKee, Carl Landau, Michael Levin, Joe Pulizzi, Brad Ring, Mark Schaefer, Jeremy Spurr, Becca Vaclavik, and Nicholas White.

Made in the USA
Middletown, DE
21 April 2018